# Protection or Free Trade
# – the Final Battle

## T. K. WHITAKER

**IPA**
INSTITUTE OF PUBLIC
ADMINISTRATION

First published 2006
Institute of Public Administration
57–61 Lansdowne Road
Dublin 4
Ireland

ISBN – 13: 978 1 904541 43 1
ISBN – 10: 1 904541 43 7

**British Library Cataloguing-in-Publication Data**
A catalogue record for this book is available from the British Library.

Cover design by Slick Fish Design
Typeset in 10.5/12 New Baskerville by Alan Hodgson
Printed in Ireland, by Future Print, Dublin

# Contents

## Publisher's Note

*Protection or Free Trade – the Final Battle* is intended to inaugurate a new series 'Issues in Public Administration'. From time to time the IPA will publish research papers and 'case material' on policy analysis and decision-making in public services. It is intended that this series will provide new and valuable insights into the management of public affairs and, thereby, help ensure higher standards and better practice in public administration and public management.

It is a happy coincidence that the first publication in the series, *Protection or Free Trade – the Final Battle*, occurs in the run-up to the ninetieth birthday of T.K. Whitaker, the central participant in the forceful exchange of semi-official correspondence which influenced a radical change of policy – Ireland's transition from protection to free trade.

*Protection or Free Trade – the Final Battle* is published in association with the Whitaker School of Government and Management.

# 1 The background

The state which achieved independence in 1922 was predominantly agricultural and relatively poor, with average incomes less than one-half of those in Britain. The population of 3.25 million included a workforce of 1.25 million, over half of whom, to put it neutrally, were "on the land". Of the 670,000 persons described statistically as being "engaged in agriculture" many were so-called "relatives assisting" on farms too small to afford them gainful employment. These "relatives assisting" formed a reservoir of hopeless, poverty-stricken underemployment which filled the emigrant ships for decades, dwarfing the gains in industrial employment which began to be made from the late 1920s onwards.[1]

The new state was in touch with the rest of the world through emigration rather than through exports, all but 2% of which went to the UK. Only one person was employed in industry for every eleven said to be "engaged" in agriculture.

The problem which confronted and baffled the early Irish governments was to secure, in a small economy with a large agricultural sector, the availability of employment at an acceptable income for all who wished to stay at home. The objective was to bring involuntary emigration to an end. In brief, the policies followed for the first thirty-six years ranged from tentative interference with inherited free trade up to 1932, to extensive and indiscriminate protection subsequently.

The two main ruling parties of this whole period were joint inheritors of the Sinn Féin (self-sufficiency) idealism of Arthur Griffith, himself a disciple of Friedrich List, but the prior attention of the earlier administration had to be given to quelling a civil war, repairing the infrastructural damage consequent on this and long years of disturbed conditions, and confirming the financial soundness and respectability of the new state. A few moderate tariffs were imposed after

---

1  This chapter includes material from chapters 1 and 3 of *Interests* (IPA 1983)

careful inquiry. The Electricity Supply Board and a sugar-beet industry were established, reducing somewhat our dependence on imports. However, there was a gain of only 5,000 new jobs in transportable goods industries between 1926 and 1931. Emigration continued to lower the population.

The 1930s saw a much more active interventionism. The advent of a new government to power in 1932 set the stage for a vigorous policy of protection and industrialisation. A financial dispute with the UK invited retaliatory recourse by both parties to tariffs and quotas. Internationally also, the trend of events was running against free trade and in favour of resort to national protectionism. The new government's protectionist policy was geared primarily towards self-sufficiency rather than the encouragement of new industry from outside. There was concern that industry should be Irish-controlled, a policy reflected in the Control of Manufactures Acts and the setting up of state-controlled monopolies in sugar and cement and a state-owned airline. In agriculture, self-sufficiency in wheat and beet and tillage generally was encouraged in preference to beef and milk production.

Protection was granted rather freely and with little scientific measurement of what was needed in individual cases. The heated atmosphere of retaliation was not conducive to any careful adjustment of aid to need. A few figures will give an idea of the zeal with which what Professor Meenan has called "the last surviving example of a predominantly free-trading state" was transformed into one of the most highly protected in the world.[2] At the end of 1931 – before the Fianna Fáil administration came to power – the list of tariffs covered 68 articles. In 1932 alone successive rounds of tariff increases brought in 67 new classes of goods at ad valorem duties ranging from 15% to 75%. Every year from then to 1938 saw high and wide-ranging duties, ad valorem or specific, imposed on previously free imports. Tariffs on intermediate products piled up to create a pyramid of protection for some final products.

---

2 J.F. Meenan, *The Irish Economy Since 1922,* Liverpool University Press, 1970, p. 142.

Professor Louden Ryan's measurement of the mounting height of the tariff wall shows that, for a representative list of commodities which bore no duty in 1924, the tariff level index in 1931 was 9% but had risen to 45% by 1936, the year which set the high-water mark of protection.[3] In that year a Coal-Cattle Pact eased the Anglo-Irish dispute, which was finally settled by the Trade Agreement of 1938, the provisions of which included machinery for review of protective duties and other import restrictions. Some tariffs were reduced or abolished in the 1936–38 period with the result that Professor Ryan's index for 1938 is down to 35%. It is to be noted, however, that the index does not measure the protective effect of the numerous quota restrictions. *The Economist* calculated in 1938 that 1,947 articles were subject to restriction or control in the state.

We should remind ourselves that protectionism was not an Irish aberration of the 1930s. The world at large was in the grip of depression; the prices of primary products had plummeted, the demand for goods had fallen catastrophically, unemployment was severe and widespread. In 1931 the new government in England announced its intention of imposing a tariff – the first general British tariff since the 1850s – and of protecting British agriculture. The practical and theoretical considerations supporting free trade were thus undermined and no inhibition lay in the way of a policy of protection aimed at securing self-sufficiency. No less an economist than Keynes spoke out in favour of such a move at University College, Dublin, in April 1933 declaring that "if I were an Irishman I should find much to attract me in the economic outlook of your present government towards self-sufficiency".[4] The extent to which free trade had been abandoned before World War II is indicated by a table in Professor Ryan's paper which shows that, taking Ireland's tariff level as 100, the level for Britain was 65, for the United States 55, for Switzerland 70 and for Germany 152.

The indiscriminate granting of protection did encourage a rapid development of low-technology industry catering almost

---

3  W.J.L. Ryan, "Measurement of Tariff Levels in Ireland", *Journal of the Statistical and Social Inquiry Society of Ireland,* 1948–49
4  First Finlay Lecture by J.M. Keynes, published in *Studies,* June 1983

exclusively for the home market. By 1936 there were 101,000 people employed in transportable goods industries, nearly twice as many as a decade before. Even during the 1930s, however, there were signs that protected industries catering only for the home market were no long-term solution for Ireland's employment problem. Gaining the wider openings in export markets on which any significant expansion of Irish industry depended would require a high level of productivity to be achieved in order to offset the cost handicap involved in both importing raw materials and exporting the final products. The industries which had been set up under protection required a substantial import content and this, without corresponding export buoyancy, could cause trouble on the external payments front. This difficulty, indeed, proved to be one of the great constraints on development policy so long as agriculture was the main source of exports and agricultural produce had to be consigned to the British market where prices were deliberately held at a low level and even access at times was not assured.

The Second World War caused scarcities and postponed any widening of the Irish industrial base. Tariffs were largely suspended during the war, industrial output fell and net output in agriculture rose. For a time after the war emigration fell slightly below the rate of natural increase but this tendency towards a rise in population was sharply reversed in the 1950s. In 1946 there were 116,000 people employed in transportable goods industries and the numbers engaged in agriculture had fallen from the 670,000 of 1926 to 594,000. Entering the 1950s exports of manufactured goods were, however, only 6% of total exports, a long way short of the contribution of agriculture.

As supplies became more freely available in the post-war period protective duties were gradually revived but with less conviction as to their efficacy as an instrument of development. In this respect, the focus was shifting to public capital expenditure as the mainspring of economic expansion. The shortcomings of an uncritical protectionist policy were being recognised, particularly its cost and price effects and the complacency and inefficiency it induced. The chief protagonist of protection, Seán Lemass, who was for many years Minister for Industry and

Commerce, war-time Minister for Supplies, and later Taoiseach in Fianna Fáil governments, came to an early realisation after the war that more effective measures were needed to set the economy on the path of competitive efficiency and growth. Although his 1947 Industrial Efficiency and Prices Bill was never enacted, it was clear evidence of his concern; and it can be seen as a precursor of the more comprehensive measures of industrial survey, tripartite consultative and advisory machinery, grants for modernisation and adaptation and even unilateral reduction of protection which he put into effect in the early 1960s after the state had first applied for membership of the EEC.

Not only Lemass, but his Labour Party counterpart in the coalition government of 1954–57, William Norton, promised comprehensive tariff reviews but, as Professor Meenan noted, no observable consequences followed and protection was, indeed, intensified, though not deliberately, in the period 1956–58 by special charges intended to discourage imports and rectify a serious imbalance in external payments. During most of the 1950s, in fact, the risk of heavy balance-of-payments deficits was a serious constraint on development policies. Recurrent sterling crises also brought pressure on sterling area countries to curb imports and internal demand in order to avert a devaluation. Agricultural exports were still the predominant source of our foreign earnings and they were subject to many vicissitudes, including unfavourable British pricing policies. It was not, indeed, until 1969 that industrial exports exceeded agricultural exports for the first time. The external deficits seemed at times quite menacing – the 1951 deficit was almost 15% of GNP – and their absolute amounts could quickly exhaust the external reserves then directly held by the Central Bank, as distinct from the commercial banks. It was not until the 1960s, and the appearance on the world scene of the Eurodollar – a product of US trade deficits – that foreign borrowing on any significant scale became possible.

In any case, the instrument by which expansion would have been sought in the early and mid-1950s – the Public Capital Programme – was itself rather ineffective; the dominance of infrastructural and social (as distinct from more immediately productive) elements in the Programme gave a low output return for the capital investment. New policy orientations were needed which would bring private enterprise and initiative into play on a bigger scale.

Despite the difficulties, the despondency and the poor economic performance (less than 2% annually by way of growth rate) of those years, the foundations of new policies for economic growth were being laid and the appropriate institutions established. In the early 1950s the Industrial Development Authority, Bord Fáilte, and Córas Tráchtála, had been set up. The industrial grants system, introduced in 1952, was extended in 1956. Tax reliefs for exports were introduced in that year by the Minister for Finance, Gerard Sweetman, who emphasised the need for "a substantial increase in volume and efficiency of national production".

Nevertheless, the years 1955–56 had plumbed the depths of hopelessness. One of the recurring balance-of-payments crises was overcome but only at the cost of stagnation, high unemployment and emigration. The mood of despondency was palpable. Something had to be done or the achievement of national independence would prove to have been a futility. Various attempts were made to shine a beam forward in this dark night of the soul; they at least agreed on the need to devote more resources on an orderly basis to productive investment.

Here, with apologies, I have to join the story in person. Born in 1916, I had entered the Department of Finance as an Administrative Officer in 1938. As an external student, i.e. by private study, I obtained a BSc(Econ) of London University in 1943, to be followed some years later by an MSc(Econ). During the war years I took part in discussions at the Statistical and Social Inquiry Society on the Beveridge Report and the implications of Keynes for monetary and employment policy. I read a paper to the Society on "Ireland's External Assets" – a First-World-War accumulation of sterling which some politicians were targeting for "repatriation". I began drafting budget speeches in 1950. Shortly before being appointed Secretary of the Department of Finance in May 1956, I read a paper to the Society entitled "Capital Formation, Saving and Economic Progress" which emphasised the need for more productive investment to help take us into an economic upswing. Later that year, the Capital Investment Advisory Committee, under the chairmanship of John Leydon, former Secretary of the Departments of Industry and Commerce and of Supplies, was set up by the Department of Finance. I kept in touch with Professor Louden Ryan and the other two professional economists on the Committee, Professors Charles Carter and Paddy Lynch.

It became clear quickly that a broader review was necessary, covering the whole field of economic activity. The basic policies of agricultural self-sufficiency and industrial protectionism needed critical examination. This was indicated in the May 1957 budget speech in words I inserted referring to the need "for a comprehensive review of our economic policy". I had started on this review, with the help of Charlie Murray of the Taoiseach's Department and Maurice Doyle and others of my own department and had made substantial progress before I wrote, towards the end of 1957, a minute to the minister, Dr James Ryan, seeking his blessing. He sent this minute to the government which endorsed his approval of the project, which was completed in May 1958 under the title *Economic Development* and published in November of that year, together with a White Paper entitled *First Programme of Economic Expansion*, largely based upon it.

Those who collaborated in producing *Economic Development* are named towards the end of the first chapter. My part was to initiate, direct, and edit it and to take responsibility for the advice and recommendations. I myself wrote chapters 1 to 4, 12 and 24 and I had the benefit of the views and encouragement of friends in the OECD, the IMF and World Bank, as well as of the three economists already mentioned, to whom I sent the draft of my first chapter.

That the new version of policy was called a "programme" (rather than a "plan") reveals the contemporary fear and distrust of the Russian type of planned economy. We were aware of course

[9]

of less objectionable precedents, such as French planning, the Vanoni plan in Italy, and the Tennessee Valley Authority in the United States. The (for us) ominous background was the movement towards free trade in Europe which Britain was likely to join – to our detriment unless we were ready to join too. We were animated by the realisation that there would never be any improvement in the then standard of living, if emigration were to cease but the current rate of increase of real output were not raised.

The First Programme changed the direction of policy, co-ordinated the development process, and gave a fillip to public confidence which, supported by buoyant world conditions, generated an outstanding economic performance in the 1960s. The GNP per capita, which in 1951 was only 55% of that in the UK, had by 1971 been lifted to 72%. The change in traditional policy was fundamental. Not only, to simplify a little, did the Programme, recognising comparative advantage, put grass before grain, but, on the industrial side, put export-oriented development, even if financed and directed by foreign entrepreneurs, before dependence on protected domestic enterprise affording only low "added-value".

The Programme's rejection of the old-fashioned protectionism was explicit:

> It would be unrealistic, in the light of the probable emergence of a Free Trade Area, to rely on a policy of protection similar to that applied over the past 25 years or so .... the only scope for substantial expansion lies in the production of goods for sale on export markets ...

The European Economic Community had come into being as a common market of six nations in 1958. The wider Free Trade Area mentioned in the Programme was mooted but never came to pass. It had less interest for us because, unlike the EEC, it had no agricultural support element. Neither had the European Free Trade Area (EFTA) comprising Britain, the Nordic Countries and Portugal. No attractive free-trade door being open, faith in free trade was in danger of being lost.

# 2 The semi-official correspondence

The correspondence reproduced here, dating from October 1959 to January 1960, is called "semi-official", a term applied to an exchange of letters between officials posing questions or arguments. The semi-official letter is a public service art-form inherited from the British régime. It is used, at various administrative levels, to supplement discussion by telephone, face-to-face, or in committee, of undecided issues. It is distinct from the "minute", a term which applies to a record of a meeting or conversation, to a submission within a Department, and to a formal letter, conveying a proposal or decision, and signed only by senior officers. Another official art-form – the memorandum – is also illustrated here.

In my time, Irish semi-official letters followed British practice in being addressed to a surname only – Dear MacCarthy, Dear Whitaker. Only very seldom was a first name used. In the correspondence reproduced here there is one example: in a letter sent on Christmas Eve 1959, we find MacCarthy, yielding to the spirit of goodwill, and writing to "Dear Ken"! In those days messengers were addressed by their Christian names, whereas an Assistant Secretary would phone "Whitaker, would you slip across, please".

The material presented here consists mainly of exchanges between the Departmental Secretaries who functioned as an advisory committee on trade policy, reporting to a Cabinet Committee comprising the Taoiseach (Seán Lemass) and the Ministers for Finance, Industry and Commerce, Agriculture, and Foreign Affairs. The letters were intended especially for the eyes of the Taoiseach when, as 1959 drew to a close, no international context was available in which benefit could be secured in return for dismantling our protective tariffs – no attractive new horizon was in view offering release from an outmoded protectionism and excessive dependence, for both industrial and agricultural exports, on the British market. We could contemplate joining the European Economic Community of six nations only if Britain joined, and EFTA – the European Free Trade Area of Britain, the Nordic countries and Portugal – offered little attraction.

I know of no better illustration of the quality, style and cogency of semi-official correspondence than is presented in this sequence of letters. I believe that, as in my own case, the letters were composed, as well as signed, by the various Secretaries of Departments. The sequence can be viewed as the final phase in the battle against the unduly prolonged espousal of "Sinn Féin" – of high protection for native industry, preclusion of foreign investment and control, and agricultural self-sufficiency – as the state's economic as well as political ideal.

**Editorial note**
With one exception the letters and other documents presented here are in chronological order as despatched. The exception is the memorandum beginning on page 25 which was prepared by the Department of Industry and Commerce and circulated in mid-October 1959, a few weeks before the series of correspondence included here was initiated. Its relevance to the central theme explored here will be evident.

The general style, capitalisation, punctuation, etc are left as found in the originals. Spelling mistakes where found are silently corrected and words underlined for emphasis in the originals are italicised.

A few footnotes refer to documents "not printed": these signify documents of a routine character or documents that repeated information already included.

# 3 The final battle

*M. Ó Muimhneacháin[5] to T.K. Whitaker, J.C.B. MacCarthy, J.C. Nagle and C.C. Cremin with draft note entitled "Anglo-Irish Trade Talks" attached, 25 November 1959*

Dear

In connection with an informal press conference which he is to hold on the 27th instant, the Taoiseach has prepared the attached note on the European Free Trade Association and the Anglo-Irish trade talks. He would be glad to have any comments you may desire to offer on the draft.

The understanding will be that the newspaper representatives will be at liberty to use the note – in its final form – as a basis for comment which will be published without any indication that it is derived from statements made by the Taoiseach or emanating from any official source. The Taoiseach is, of course, anxious that what is published should be helpful from our point of view and should be free from inaccuracy on any material point.

It would be appreciated if you could let me have your observations – in triplicate – not later than tomorrow afternoon, the 26th instant.

I am writing in the same terms to

M. Ó MUIMHNEACHÁIN

Sent to/

T.K. Whitaker, Esq.,
Secretary, Department of Finance.

J.C.B. McCarthy, Esq.,
Secretary, Department of Industry & Commerce.

J.C. Nagle, Esq.,
Secretary, Department of Agriculture.

C.C. Cremin, Esq.,
Secretary, Department of External Affairs.

---

5 Maurice Moynihan (1902–99), Secretary, Department of the Taoiseach (1937–60), later Governor of the Central Bank of Ireland (1961–69)

DRAFT
## Anglo-Irish Trade Talks

Q.: Would the Taoiseach give some briefing on the Anglo-Irish Trade talks?

A.: With the conclusion of the Stockholm negotiations for a European Free Trade Association, it is to be assumed that the resumption of the Anglo-Irish trade negotiations will be arranged for a comparatively early date, possibly during December. It was the Irish view that it would not be desirable to press for the resumption of the trade talks before the completion of the Stockholm negotiations.

The European Free Trade Association agreement has produced few surprises, being generally in the form anticipated in newspaper forecasts. The members of E.F.T.A. contract to eliminate tariffs and quotas, as between themselves, by January 1st, 1969. Portugal has secured exceptional treatment to the extent that industries which are not export industries need not be completely deprived of protection in the home market for twenty years, although, in the case of these industries, tariffs must be reduced by 50% in ten years. Export industries are defined as those industries which exported more than 15% of their production on the average during each of the three years to December 1958. Portugal also secured the right to impose new tariffs to foster new industries which must not be higher than the average level of tariffs in force in Portugal at the time, and be subject to the over-riding obligation to dispense with all tariffs in twenty years.

It is considered that the Portuguese arrangements would not have been applicable to the circumstances of Ireland if we had been involved in the negotiations, and should the question of Ireland joining the E.F.T.A. arise at any time, it is certain that different arrangements would be sought in closer accord with Irish conditions. The agreement provides that, subject to the approval of the Council of E.F.T.A., another State, such as Ireland, may accede to the agreement on such terms and conditions as may be decided.

[18]

The view is strongly held here, however, that joining the E.F.T.A. would confer no benefit on this country. The prospects of increasing export trade to the seven member States to compensate for higher imports of industrial products from them are thought to be remote.

Irish interest is mainly in the agricultural provisions of the Stockholm agreement. The tariff and quota removal obligations do not apply to agricultural goods, but tariff reductions granted by one member to another under the bilateral agreements made prior to the main agreement (i.e. the Anglo-Danish agreement) shall apply to the products of all members. Export subsidies shall not be granted by any member for the purpose of increasing that member's share of any agricultural trade within the area.

The provisions relating to agricultural products, of greater significance to this country, are those which refer to possibilities of action against dumped or subsidised products. If a member State complains that she is suffering from or threatened with material injury to her trade as a result of the export of dumped or subsidised products into the market of another member, by a country outside the agreement, the country whose market is affected in that way is obliged to "examine the possibility of taking such action as is consistent with its international obligations to remedy the injury". Probably the interpretation of this clause, and its applicability to Anglo-Irish trade, will be one of the matters in which the Irish negotiators will seek clarification in the resumed trade talks.

There does not appear to be anything in the E.F.T.A. agreement which would involve any revision of the existing Anglo-Irish trade agreement, or preclude the possibility of an extension of that agreement as, it is understood, the Irish representatives proposed in the previous talks in London.

*T.K. Whitaker[6] to M. Ó Muimhneacháin with document attached entitled "Department of Finance Comments on Draft Note on European Free Trade Area and Anglo-Irish Trade Talks", 26 November 1959*

Dear Ó Muimhneacháin,
I enclose herewith some comments on the draft note on the European Free Trade Association and the Anglo-Irish Trade talks which you forwarded with your letter of 25 November.

I would like to emphasise the necessity for suspending judgement on the acceptability of the Portuguese arrangements in our circumstances until the matter has been fully examined in the light of recent developments. There is no doubt that ideas about the speed of transition are now much more ambitious, both in the Six and the Seven, than they were when the Seventeen were negotiating. The 15% rule would mean that very few of our industries – and these the strongest – would have to eliminate tariffs in less than twenty years. In any case, the tempo of Working Party No. 23 terms is now made to appear very slow and unrealistic.

Quite apart from free trade developments, I believe firmly in the need for systematic tariff reductions here as one of the ways of ensuring improvement in industrial efficiency and expansion of exports. I have set out before the grounds for this belief. The arrangements now made by thirteen of the more industrialised European countries to dismantle tariffs and increase mutual trade – and the possibility of this being completed in seven or ten years – make it more difficult but at the same time more urgently necessary for us to become competitive over a wider field. Only formal "free trade" arrangements with Britain, or a group including Britain, can provide the necessary drive and discipline on the industrial side as well as some prospect of gain on the agricultural side. One could not contemplate, without grave disquiet, the possibility of our remaining in what I have described as "unprogressive isolation".

---

6 Secretary, Department of Finance

I know that even a gradual withdrawal of protection will create difficulties for some industries but, on the whole, I am encouraged by the confident and progressive reaction to greater freedom of trade expressed in the recent pamphlet of the National Council of the Federation of Irish Industries –

> "The National Council is confident that Irish industry in general is sufficiently strong and adaptable not only to meet the situation but also to develop and prosper, provided that action is taken in time by individual firms and by industries and that the co-operation and the assistance of the Government is forthcoming."

At the next meeting with the British we may find that the "favourable discrimination" half of our proposals cannot be accepted, in which event we shall have to consider what is the best bargain we can make with the "free trade" half. A reading of the F.I.I. pamphlet suggests that it might be advisable to associate representatives of the Federation of Irish Industries, the N.F.A. and the Irish Trade Union Congress with the formulation of a revised initiative.

I am sending a copy of this letter and enclosure to MacCarthy, Nagle and Cremin.

Yours sincerely,
T.K. WHITAKER

## DEPARTMENT OF FINANCE COMMENTS ON DRAFT NOTE ON EUROPEAN FREE TRADE AREA AND ANGLO-IRISH TRADE TALKS[7]

Page 1, 1st Par. of Answer [page 18, first paragraph of answer]:
The validity – and value – of the second sentence is doubtful and it might be deleted. The delay is probably due more to other causes. Against the explanation advanced here, it could be argued that our interest lay in having the British committed as much as possible to us before conclusions at Stockholm restricted their freedom of action.

Page 1, 2nd Par., line 6 [page 18, second paragraph of answer, line 5]:
Substitute "1970" for "1969".

Page 1, last sentence on page [page 18, second paragraph of answer, last sentence]:
After "right" insert "up to 1 July, 1972, to increase existing duties or".

Page 2, 1st Par. [page 18, third paragraph of answer]:
It would seem premature to decide emphatically at this stage that the Portuguese arrangements would not be applicable to the circumstances of Ireland, although we would doubtless seek more favourable arrangements in the first instance.

Page 2, 2nd Par., 1st Sentence [page 19, first paragraph, first sentence]:
It is suggested that this sentence be toned down. There are long-term benefits, for instance:-

(1) The discipline of progressive tariff reduction would operate to bring about increased efficiency and reduced costs in Irish industry which would improve the prospects of expansion of Irish exports not only to Britain and the other members of EFTA but also to other countries.

---

7 Owing to the new layout of the original draft on pages 18–19, the locations referred to in the original shoulder notes have changed. The new locations are noted within square brackets.

(2) Membership of EFTA would help to attract foreign industrialists to establish enterprises here.

(3) By joining the same free trade area as Britain (which has obligations under GATT) we would be in a better position to obtain favourable treatment from Britain.

Page 2, 2nd Par., 2nd Sentence [page 19, first paragraph, second sentence]:
It is also desirable to modify this sentence which, since Britain is one of the Seven, seems to discount even the possibility of increased agricultural exports to Britain.

Page 2, 3rd Par. [page 19, second paragraph]:
In view of comments on 2nd paragraph the first sentence might be deleted.

Page 3, 1st Par. [page 19, third paragraph]:
It is suggested that the words "of greater significance to this country" in the first sentence should be deleted. Generally, it is for consideration whether, having referred to the anti-subsidy rule, we should not take the line that we do not think it applicable to Anglo-Irish trade. The present wording seems to imply that we feel vulnerable on this point.

General:
Further observations are contained in a semi-official covering letter to Mr. Ó Muimhneacháin.[8]

---

8 See pages 20–21.

## J.C.B. MacCarthy[9] to T.K. Whitaker, 26 November 1959

Dear Whitaker,

I have seen the copy which you kindly sent me of the letter addressed to Ó Muimhneacháin to-day in connection with the draft note for the Taoiseach's Press Conference on the European Free Trade Association.

There is one statement in that letter which surprises us here namely that "the 15% rule would mean that very few of our industries – and these the strongest – would have to eliminate tariffs in less than 20 years". I am afraid this is not a generalisation which we could accept. It will not do just to take the industries on a numerical basis; one has to have regard to employment and relative importance. As you will see from the statement attached,[10] which we prepared when we were considering how the Portuguese arrangements would work out if applied to us, the 15% rule would immediately hit industries providing a very large percentage of our industrial employment. I think a glance at page 1 of the statement will convince you at once of this.

We sent you copies of this statement with our memorandum on the Outer Seven on the 14th October.[11]

Yours sincerely,
(J.C.B. MacCARTHY)

---

9 James Charles Brendan MacCarthy (1908–90), Secretary, Department of Industry and Commerce. Following his retirement in 1972 he joined the boards of several prominent companies in Ireland.
10 Not printed
11 See document following

*Memorandum referred to in MacCarthy's letter on page 24. It was prepared in October 1959 by the Department of Industry and Commerce and dealt with the implications for Irish industry of joining the Free Trade Association of the Outer Seven.*

## IRELAND AND THE OUTER SEVEN

1. The Department of Industry and Commerce have been examining the possible effect on Irish industry of our joining the European Free Trade Association of the Outer Seven (U.K., Norway, Sweden, Denmark, Austria, Switzerland, Portugal). At the commencement of the European Free Trade Area discussions in 1956 the Department examined the effects which the removal of industrial protection against all O.E.E.C. countries would have, and concluded that the result would be nothing less than the undoing of thirty years of industrial development. The measure of the jobs that would be lost in industry is given in Appendix II to the Interim Report of the Committee of Secretaries, submitted to the Government early in 1957, as 100,000, a figure which would be reduced by about 20,000 if the food, drink and tobacco industries were excluded from the Free Trade Area. In the light of this estimate it was decided that in the event of our joining a Free Trade Area of all O.E.E.C. countries, we should seek a period of years during which we would be exempt from obligations to scale down protection and thereafter given a long transitional period. The principle of this request, which was made early in the Paris negotiations, was accepted, and some time before the Inter-Governmental Committee suspended the negotiations, they "expressed general agreement" with a set of proposals, under which, among other things, Ireland would have a transitional period twice as long as that of the developed countries and would be required during the first ten years to make tariff reductions amounting to only 10% in all.

2. A study of the Stockholm Plan for the Association of the Outer Seven shows that the conclusions reached in regard to the Free Trade Area are broadly valid also in the case of the Outer Seven, as far as the consequences of membership for Irish industry are concerned. It is true that, initially at least, the new grouping would not include the Common Market countries, some of which are large exporters of industrial goods. It is to be expected, however, that ultimately there will be some form of association between the Six and the Outer Seven and that each group will share in the tariff reductions etc. of the other. Also, the scale of tariff reductions and quota enlargements negotiated at Stockhom provides for total dismantlement of protection by 1970, while under the Rome Treaty, which in this respect was the model for the Draft Convention for a Free Trade Area, the process might not be completed until 1973.

3. The possibility of Ireland being offered membership of the Outer Seven on the terms sought by Portugal has been mentioned. The main feature of these terms is that exporting industries only would bear the full tariff reductions; non-exporting industries would be permitted to reduce tariffs at one-half the rate, until in 1970 the level of protection remaining for those industries would be one-half of the present level. The remaining half would be abolished at a rate to be fixed later. A difficulty arises from the fact that an exporting industry has not been defined. Information received from British sources is that the Portuguese have been thinking in terms of an industry exporting 15% of production but that the British delegation at Stockholm think that any industry exporting 10% or more of its output should bear the tariff reductions to be generally applied.

4. Attached to this memorandum is a table showing our industries in order of percentage of output exported. This table shows that 11 groups of industry, employing over 32,000 workers, export 15% or more of production, while six further groups employing another 33,000 export between 10% and 15% of their output. These 17 categories include our main protected industries, viz. leather, clothing, footwear, woollen and worsted and other textiles, printing

and publishing, paper and board and electrical machinery, etc. It is evident that we could not contemplate the abolition of the tariffs on these goods over the next 10 or 11 years.

5. There is another possibility to be considered, and that is that the British would agree that the tariff reductions to be carried out by us in the Outer Seven would apply only to the Full rates until these were reduced to the Preferential rates. This would represent a big concession by the British not only to us, but to their partners as well; presumably it would be proposed only as part of a very wide settlement. The elimination of British preferences in our market, which would be involved, would of course also mean the elimination of our case for a quid pro quo from Britain.

6. Application of the Portuguese formula to the Full rates only from the beginning would bring the full rates down to the Preferential level by January 1962 in the case of an exporting industry, and by January 1967 in the case of a non-exporting industry. The latter group, if the criterion taken is an industry exporting less than 10% of output, would include hosiery, shirtmaking, cotton, chemicals, paints, wood, fertilisers. Total employment in protected industries exporting less than 10% of output is in the region of 50,000.

7. Assuming that we would be offered membership on Portuguese terms, taking a 10% export as the dividing line between an exporting and a non-exporting industry, and assuming further that we could apply tariff reductions to the Full rates only until these approximated to the Preferential rates, the position would be that the tariff against Britain would be unaffected until 1968 in the case of a non-exporting industry whereas the exporting industries, employing some 65,000 workers directly, would have to take cuts in the tariff against Britain as from 1963, the tariff being eliminated in their case by 1970.

8. In some cases the most serious competition for our industries comes from Britain and it could be expected that they would not be materially affected until the rate on British goods came to be reduced. It should be noted, however, that there

are some industries e.g. paper and board (employment 4,800), hosiery (5,900), electrical machinery (1,400) in which competition from the Continental members of the Outer Seven would result in increased exports to Ireland at a very early stage, when the Full rates were being reduced.

9. There would be no postponement of effective tariff reductions for industries protected by flat rates of duty e.g. aluminium goods, cables, veneer and plywood, woollen and worsted yarns.

10. Mention must be made of the industries protected by quota, which employ over 22,000. The Portuguese formula seeks no special treatment on quotas, so that the protection given to the woollen and worsted, footwear, tyres and tubes, and other industries would have to be very seriously whittled down through substantial quota increases from next year on, and completely abolished by 1970.

11. When compared with the treatment we might have, with reluctance, accepted in a Free Trade Area of all O.E.E.C. countries, the Stockholm Plan, as adapted by the Portuguese formula, even when that formula is applied to the full rates of duty only from the beginning, is distinctly more onerous for Irish industry.

12. Turning to possible opportunities which a lowering of barriers against Irish exports to the Outer Seven would open up, it must be stated first that all but £1.6m. of our £17.8m. export trade to Britain in industrial items last year qualified for free entry, almost all of the £1.6m. getting a tariff preference over goods of the other members of the Outer Seven. In addition to the tariff advantage nearly £4m. of our exports benefited from the operation of British quotas against the other Outer Seven countries. We have already estimated a loss of £4m. worth of industrial trade to Britain on Britain's joining the Outer Seven. The question arises whether this can be made good in exports to other countries of the Stockholm group. As will be seen from a statement attached our exports to those countries in 1958 amounted only to £1m. Nearly half consisted of beef and veal and other agricultural items, while raw materials

like scrap, ores and wool made up a quarter. The most important industrial items were plaster boards (£94,000), motor cars (£33,000) and textiles (£21,000). The prospects of increasing exports to those countries, in these or other industrial items on a reduction of tariffs and enlargement of quotas there, are not encouraging.

13. There is an important point to bear in mind when considering terms of membership of the Outer Seven. It is now apparent that strenuous efforts will be made to link the Common Market with the Seven. If we show inclination to join the latter group on the Portuguese terms, we will find it impossible later to restore our position even to that which we held at the later meetings of Working Party No. 23 and which we would regard as one creating difficulties enough for our manufacturers. Any tariff reductions made in favour of the Outer Seven would have to be extended to the Six in the event of an association being concluded between the two groups, and competition from the Six would be far more serious than competition from the Continental members of the Outer Seven.

14. The foregoing paragraphs show that the special terms sought by Portugal under the Stockholm arrangement are considerably less favourable than those which we might have accepted in the Paris negotiations. It was only with great difficulty that Ireland could see her way to agree to join a Free Trade Area of the "Seventeen" on the special conditions drawn up in Working Party No. 23. Joining the Area, even with these conditions, involved the abolition of our industrial protection in the long run and was something which could only be contemplated in the light of the facts that otherwise we would be completely isolated and also that there was a fair prospect that in a Free Trade Area of 250 millions, Ireland would be able to increase exports of one kind or another, particularly agricultural exports, and so help to counterbalance the losses sustained through ultimate abolition of protection.

15. In the Stockholm Free Trade Association, however, there do not appear to be any prospects that the losses

suffered through the abolition of our protection would be counterbalanced by advantages gained from joining this group. There is a market of only 88 million people in the countries forming the group and of this Britain accounts for over 50 millions. We have almost complete duty free entry into Britain at the moment, so that the only commercial advantage to be gained from joining the Area is free entry to a market of 38 million which is largely constituted by small countries like ourselves (e.g. Norway, Denmark and Austria) with somewhat similar economies and substantially agricultural. There does not seem to be much hope that Irish goods would find any substantial outlet in these markets which would compensate for the influx of goods, not only from these countries but also from Britain, which would follow abolition of our protection.

16. Therefore, unless it is desirable for political reasons or unless (notwithstanding the possible weakening of our tactical position) it is considered necessary as a stepping stone to membership on special terms of a wider Free Trade Area of all O.E.E.C. countries, assuming that such an Area would be formed, there appears to be little case for contemplating joining the Outer Seven.

17. The various aspects of the Stockholm Plan have been examined in the Department. In some minor respects, e.g. Rules of Competition, the Plan is less onerous than the Free Trade Area proposals. However, none of these features is of sufficient importance to justify a revision of the general conclusion contained in the preceding paragraph.

18. Three statements[12] are attached showing
    1. Imports from the Outer Seven (other than Britain)
    2. Exports to the Outer Seven (other than Britain)
    3. Industries, showing proportion of output exported, etc.

12 Not printed

*T.K. Whitaker to C. Murray,[13] 27 November 1959*

## FREE TRADE

Mr. Murray,
The diehard Industry and Commerce contention that joining EFTA (and presumably any other free trade area) would be of no economic benefit to this country would seem to apply with as much validity to, say, Sweden. Underlying the contention is the view that the advantage of freer trade for any country in terms of improved access to export markets would be counterbalanced by improved access of the other partners to that country's home market. If this were so, it is hard to see how any group of countries would ever join in a free trade area. The argument leaves out of account the *general* prospect of increased sales resulting from keener competition, increased efficiency and greater specialisation.

We have already (in letters and in the course of memoranda) contested the Industry & Commerce opposition to freer trade (which does not seem to cause anything like as much alarm to the Federation of Irish Industries) but I think the time is ripe for the preparation of a reasoned memorandum directed specifically towards setting out, without exaggeration, the reasons in favour of a progressive lowering of our protective tariffs in the context of a free trade area which includes Britain – and this irrespective of any improvement in our agricultural relations with Britain. This can conveniently be done as a by-product of our examination of the implications for us of joining EFTA on Portuguese terms.

Yours sincerely,
T.K. WHITAKER

---

13 Charlie Murray, Department of Finance, later Secretary of that Department.

### M. Ó Muimhneacháin to T.K. Whitaker, 27 November 1959

Dear Whitaker,

The Taoiseach desires to have a study made, in the light of the agreement concluded between the member-countries of the European Free Trade Association, of the position which will arise if the British find our proposals for improved economic relations with Britain unacceptable in their present form.

The study might be directed in particular towards suggesting answers to the following queries:-

(1) What would be the short-term and long-term implications for this country of joining the European Free Trade Association on terms similar to those agreed to in the case of Portugal?

(2) What minimum agricultural concessions from the British would be acceptable to this country in return for joining the Association?

(3) Would it be more in our interest to seek "free trade" arrangements as at (1) with Britain alone than with the Association as a whole?

(4) How far would such "free trade" arrangements with Britain be compatible with Britain's obligations to the Association and otherwise?

The Taoiseach desires to discuss these matters with the Ministers more immediately concerned and the Secretaries of their departments before the proposed meeting with British Ministers. It would be helpful if the results of a preliminary Departmental examination were incorporated in a single memorandum which could be circulated beforehand to the Taoiseach and the Ministers concerned. It is suggested that the Secretaries of the Departments concerned might consult together with a view to the early preparation of such a memorandum.

You will appreciate that the matter is one of great urgency.

I am writing in the same terms to MacCarthy, Nagle and Cremin.

Yours sincerely,

M. Ó MUIMHNEACHÁIN

## T.K. Whitaker to J.C.B. MacCarthy, 27 November 1959

Dear MacCarthy,

Thanks for your letter of 26th November about the effect on our industries of the Portuguese terms.

I have, of course, seen your statistical statement but I still consider my generalisation fair. The industries your figures indicate as being "hit" by the 15% rule include brewing (employment 4,653) and distilling (employment 645) which are not protected and should therefore be excluded. They also include motor assembly (employment 4,451) which, having regard to average exports for 1956, 1957 and 1958, would also be excluded. The remainder of the industries affected (employment 22,000) are grouped under eight rather wide headings. These will require to be subdivided into individual industries, many of which will prove to have less than 15% exports. I shall be surprised if you find that the number of workers in industries with more than 15% exports exceeds 5% to 10% of the total employed in manufacturing industry (148,000).

The more important point, however, is that the industries concerned would be those which are in fact efficient and progressive such as Irish Ropes, Waterford Glass, etc. One would expect these, in view of their export performance, to be strong enough to bear the gradual abolition of home market protection over 10 years.

Yours sincerely,
T.K. WHITAKER

cc. Mr. Ó Muimhneacháin
    Mr. Cremin
    Mr. Nagle

## J.C.B. MacCarthy to T.K. Whitaker, 1 December 1959

Dear Whitaker,

Many thanks for your letter of the 27th November on the question of the appropriateness in our situation of terms similar to those which the Portuguese are getting under EFTA.

I did not intend to include brewing and distilling because, as they are not protected, the question doesn't arise in relation to them.

I think it is quite true as you suggest that within the groups which show an overall export of more than 15%, there are some particular industries with exports of less than 15%; but I think it is conversely true that under other headings there are industries with more than 15% exports. These items would probably cancel out. There could also be a problem of segregating the industries. We have this problem in defining the scope of tariffs.

As regards your last paragraph, I am afraid that it is not safe to judge by reference to their current success in the export market, the capacity of industries to maintain themselves on the home market if protection is withdrawn. We have reason to believe that some industries maintain their export trade by charging lower prices on the export market than they do at home. It is, we believe, a common practice to charge all overheads against home sales. Furthermore, many of these industries get special duty-free import facilities for their export trades and have to use duty-paid or dearer home-produced materials for the home trade. Other points to be borne in mind are (a) that the close proximity of the British market would enable aggressive salesmanship to be adopted by British firms on a scale which is unlikely to arise as between Britain and other members of EFTA – for all practical purposes British suppliers regard this country as an extension of their home market; (b) that our newly-established industries need protection because of the wider range and variety of lines which the larger foreign industries can put on our market and (c) that the established goodwill, advertising power and trade connections of these external manufacturers and the prejudice which exists in favour of well-known imported products would make it difficult for Irish firms to secure a reasonable share of the home market even where they are competitive in quality and price.

Yours sincerely,
(J.C.B. MacCARTHY).

*T.K. Whitaker to J.C.B. MacCarthy with comments attached on the Department of Industry and Commerce Memorandum of October 1959 entitled "Ireland and the Outer Seven", 4 December 1959*

Dear MacCarthy,
I enclose observations on the memorandum, transmitted with Connolly's letter of 14th October, 1959, on the implications for Irish industry of joining EFTA. The summary referred to in the final paragraph of our observations will be available shortly.

Yours sincerely,
T.K. WHITAKER

cc. Mr. Ó Muimhneacháin
    Mr. Cremin
    Mr. Nagle

Comments on Department of Industry and Commerce
Memorandum of October, 1959,
entitled "Ireland and the Outer Seven"[14]

Paragraph 1:

The estimate that 100,000 jobs would be lost in industry following the removal of industrial protection against all OEEC countries could not be accepted without critical examination. The separate Industry and Commerce memorandum in which this estimate appeared was appended to the Report of the Committee of Secretaries at the request of that Department but the contents were not agreed by the Committee. A wide range of considerations was taken into account by the Committee in reaching the general view summarised at paragraph 20 of the Report as follows:-

> "As there is no future for our economy unless production for export can be expanded on a competitive basis, we should take no decision to stay out of the Free Trade Area until we have explored every possibility of going in with adequate safeguards as a country in process of economic development."

It would, therefore, be misleading to ascribe predominantly to any particular consideration the decision to seek special terms of admission to a free trade area.

Paragraph 2:

As indicated in the comments on paragraph 1, the Industry and Commerce views on the original Free Trade Area proposals were not generally agreed and cannot, therefore, be accepted as applying to the EFTA proposals.

As regards the grouping, it should be borne in mind that competition from Continental EFTA countries in the industrial sector would not be as strong as that of the Common Market countries, particularly Germany and Italy. Industrial enterprises in the countries of the Seven other than Britain are closer in size to those in this country than those, say, in Western Germany, Italy or France. This is recognised in Paragraph 15 of the

14 See pages 25–30

memorandum which says that the Area "is largely constituted by small countries like ourselves (e.g. Norway, Denmark and Austria) with somewhat similar economics and substantially agricultural".

In regard to the third sentence it is not certain that the establishment of EFTA will lead to some kind of association with the Common Market countries. Some commentators (cf. The Economist of 28th November, 1959) apprehend that the establishment of EFTA far from leading to a united European Free Trade Area may have the opposite effect.

As regards the suggestion that total protection might not be dismantled in the Common Market countries until 1973 as against the ten-year period of EFTA, there is now every indication that the Common Market will come into full operation before 1970. A proposal that the transition period should end in 1965 is at present being studied. There appears to be fairly general agreement that some speeding up of the transition period is likely in view of the prevailing boom conditions in the member countries.

Paragraph 3:
Under the special arrangements for Portuguese tariff reductions only goods the export of which amounts to 15% or more of production on the average of the three years ended 31st December, 1958, will have to bear the full tariff reductions within the ten-year period. In addition to being allowed double the transition period for the abolition of tariffs protecting non-exporting industries, she is being accorded the right subject to certain conditions to raise existing duties or impose duties for new industries up to 1st July, 1972. While Portugal has not been granted any special terms in respect of the relaxation of import quota restrictions, the Convention provides for special arrangements in this regard.

Paragraph 4:
Of the 11 industrial groups (employing over 32,000 workers) shown in the table as exporting 15% or more of production (on the basis of 1956 output and 1958 exports), it has been

agreed that brewing and distilling should not be included as they are not protected. This excludes 5,298 workers. Again, the motor assembly industry (employing 4,541) would not have to bear the full tariff reductions. The statement shows exports of £1,776,000 in 1958, equivalent to just 15% of 1956 output. This figure includes exports of second-hand vehicles. Even with the inclusion of these items average exports in the three years 1956-1958, which is the period stipulated in the Convention, were only 12.2% of 1956 output. As the criterion adopted for the definition of an exporting industry is the value of exports as a percentage of output, it would scarcely seem reasonable to include second-hand items. Exports of new cars, etc., were:

|                    | 1956 | 1957 | 1958 |
|--------------------|------|------|------|
|                    | £    | £    | £    |
| Motor cars         | 22,979 | 1,057,555 | 987,403 |
| Goods vehicles     | –    | 78,619 | –    |
| Motor tractors     | 3,384 | 12,235 | 13,338 |
|                    | 26,363 | 1,148,409 | 1,000,741 |
| % of 1956 output   | 0.2% | 9.6% | 8.4% |

Average 1956-1958 ..... 6%

Exports in 1959 are much below the 1958 level.

In a number of the other industrial groups listed as exporting 15% or more of production it would be found, if the descriptions were broken down, that a small number of industries would account for the bulk of the exports attributed to the group. The heading "manufacture and assembly of machinery except electrical equipment" is a case in point. This heading includes the assembly of Japanese sewing machines for export to Britain. Exports of these machines last year amounted to £169,264 as compared with exports of £16,729 for all other classes of textile machinery. In the first nine months of 1959 exports of sewing machines were valued at £569,530. In the very wide heading "jute, canvas, rayon, nylon, cordage and miscellaneous textile manufactures", exports of twine, cord, ropes and cables accounted for over £300,000 of the total exports of the group of £1,354,000. Another instance is the group "glass and glassware, pottery, china and earthenware" in which the high exports of Waterford Glass may be responsible for the percentage figure exceeding 15%. Of total exports of the group of £496,000 in 1958, exports of glassware accounted for £467,000. The position may be the same in the case of other headings, particularly in the textile and clothing groups. On the other hand, it is possible that under the group headings where exports are less than 15% of output there are some industries exporting 15% or more.

On the whole it would not appear that many industries would have to bear the full tariff reductions within ten years and that the employment in these industries would not be much more than 5 to 10% of total employment in manufacturing industries. The Central Statistics Office have been asked to prepare a detailed analysis of the position.

Paragraphs 5, 6 & 7:
It would appear from Article 3 and Annex A of the Convention that our preferential rates would have to be progressively reduced in line with the percentage reductions in the full rates. It is difficult to visualise Britain agreeing that our tariff reductions would apply only to the full rates until these were reduced to the level of the preferential rates.

The calculations in paragraphs 6 and 7 regarding industries exporting 10% of output are not now relevant.

Paragraphs 8 & 9:
Even if we were not under compulsion to reduce preferential tariffs along with full tariffs from the beginning it is likely that any increase in our imports from the continental members of EFTA in the early stages of the transition period would be at the expense of British imports, having regard to the fact that, as the Department of Industry and Commerce has contended, the preferential rate of duty is the effective rate.

In the case of industries protected by flat rates of duty there would still be some postponement of effective tariff reductions if, as appears probable, the existing rates of duty are higher than is absolutely necessary.

Paragraph 10:
While Article 10 of the Convention provides for the progressive relaxation of quotas and their elimination by 31st December, 1969, there is a proviso that if in relation to a particular product this would cause a member country serious difficulties that member may propose to the Council alternative arrangements for that product and the Council may, by majority decision, authorise alternative arrangements. It is, therefore, not necessarily the case that the protection afforded by our quotas would have to be "very seriously whittled down through substantial quota increases from next year on and completely abolished by 1970".

While Portugal has not obtained any special arrangements in regard to the relaxation of import quotas it may be that none was sought. There is a likelihood that we would obtain concessions in respect of quotas which at present protect industries exporting less than 15% of their output. In any event, we would be on fairly strong ground in requesting a concession for goods protected by quota as there does not seem to be any reason to distinguish these from goods protected by tariff.

There is the further important point, not mentioned in the memorandum, that the Convention contains an escape clause for a country encountering difficulties in particular sectors of industry. Article 20 provides that if a member experiences an appreciable rise in unemployment in a particular sector of industry or region caused by a substantial decrease in internal demand for a domestic product and this decrease in demand is due to an increase in imports from a member country as a result of the progressive elimination of duties, charges and quantitative restrictions in accordance with the Convention that member may limit these imports by quantitative restriction or take such other measures as the Council, by majority decision, may authorise.

Paragraph 11:
The most favourable terms of admission to EFTA would probably be more onerous than the now unrealistic working Party No. 23 terms. On the other hand, competition on the

home market would not be as severe as in a Free Trade Area of the Seventeen having regard to the absence of Germany, Italy, Belgium, The Netherlands and France, which have all highly developed industrial systems.

Economic expansion depends on a widening range of Irish industrial production becoming competitive in price and quality with foreign goods. The free trade arrangements already made by the major countries of Europe are designed to achieve greater specialisation, higher output and lower costs. This makes it at once more difficult and more urgently necessary for us to lower our costs sufficiently.

The gradual externally-applied discipline of tariff reductions which membership of a free trade area would entail would accelerate the achievement of greater efficiency and higher exports.

The National Council of the Federation of Irish Industries in a pamphlet entitled "European Free Trade and the Prospects for Irish Industry" issued recently for the private information and guidance of members says that:-

> "Any rational examination of the trend of events leads to the conclusion that fundamental changes in economic policies are imminent and will involve progressive reduction of protection for Irish industries leading eventually to free trade conditions. These changes will pose many serious problems for industry in Ireland but industry is capable of meeting the challenge. It can develop and prosper but only if plans are made and put into effect immediately to meet changing circumstances".

And again:–

> "The National Council is confident that Irish industry in general is sufficiently strong and adaptable not only to meet the situation but also to develop and prosper provided that action is taken in time by individual firms and by industries and that cooperation and assistance of the Government is forthcoming".

Paragraph 12:
It is Government policy at present to encourage foreign investment in this country with a view particularly to the expansion of exports. If we isolate ourselves from European trade groupings, such as EFTA, Ireland would provide less attraction for foreign industrialists.

The Department of Industry and Commerce estimate of a loss of £4 million in our industrial exports to Britain on the establishment of EFTA appears to overlook the fact that tariffs will only gradually be eliminated. We would lose a good deal less of our share of the British market for manufactured goods if we increased our competitiveness within EFTA.

While our exports to continental EFTA countries are small (about £1 million in 1958) it may be that the protective systems employed in those countries have operated to limit our exports. The external trade of those countries is relatively large: imports form 25% of national income as compared with 16% in Britain and 3% in the United States. As importers, the seven countries together are nearly one-and-a-third times as important as the American market.

Following are the figures for 1958 and the first nine months of 1959 for our external trade with continental EFTA countries:-

|  | Imports | | Domestic Exports | |
|  |  | Jan.-Sept. |  | Jan.-Sept. |
|  | 1958 | 1959 | 1958 | 1959 |
|  |  | £(000) |  |  |
| Austria | 308 | 319 | 28 | 25 |
| Denmark | 1,369 | 1,542 | 64 | 102 |
| Norway | 376 | 368 | 313 | 30 |
| Portugal | 391 | 286 | 99 | 139 |
| Sweden | 2,474 | 2,440 | 439 | 622 |
| Switzerland | 728 | 486 | 85 | 59 |
| Total: | 5,646 | 5,441 | 1,028 | 977 |

The 1959 figures to date show an expansion of exports to these countries despite the collapse of the market for our chilled and frozen beef in Norway which was valued at over £¼ million in 1958.

It is necessary to draw attention to the implications of the provisions of Article 13 of the Convention as regards the statutory reliefs from direct taxation provided by the Financial (Miscellaneous Provisions) Act, 1956, as amended, and by the Finance (Miscellaneous Provisions) Act, 1958, which were specifically designed to promote exports from this country. Those concessions give exporters 100% remission of income taxation on increased exports for a ten-year period or alternatively 25% remission of taxation on *all* exports for a five-year period. In the case of export industries established at the Shannon Customs Free Airport there is 100% remission of income taxation for 25 years.

Article 13 of the Convention requires that Member States shall not maintain or introduce various stated forms of aid to export of goods to other Member States including, inter alia, "the remission, calculated in relation to exports, of direct taxes ….. on industrial or commercial enterprises". This Article would seem to require the discontinuance of our export tax reliefs as far as exports to Member States of EFTA are concerned. (Incidentally, it may be noted that these reliefs already conflict with our OEEC obligations). The position, however, is that the State has pledged itself by statute to accord the export tax reliefs over the various periods indicated above. Manufacturing interests, home and foreign, have already undertaken projects to develop exports in the light of these pledges and the concession could not now be withdrawn without a grave breach of public faith. It would be necessary, therefore, in the event of this country's acceding to the Convention to seek a derogation from the provisions of Article 13 in respect of existing export tax reliefs.

Paragraph 13:
As mentioned under paragraph 2, there is no guarantee that a link will be forged between the Common Market and EFTA. If any association takes place between the two areas it will be very different from the Free Trade Area envisaged during Working

Party No. 23 negotiations. It is extremely unlikely that we would be accorded the terms recommended by Working Part No. 23 in any such association. Ideas about the speed of transition are now much more ambitious, both in the Six and Seven, then they were when the Seventeen were negotiating.

Paragraphs 14-16:
The conclusion in the memorandum that there appears to be little case for contemplating joining EFTA is unwarranted. The dependence of economic expansion on greater efficiency and lower costs, and the manner in which association with EFTA could assist in achieving these objectives, has been referred to briefly in the comment on paragraph 11. As it is of critical importance that all aspects of the question be considered, a separate summary is being prepared in this Department of the arguments in favour of effecting tariff reductions even apart from free trade developments in Europe and, a fortiori, of the desirability of doing so if agricultural concessions are available in return for our entering a free trade system. This summary will also advert to the implications of remaining isolated from the free trade movement in Europe.

Notes prepared by the Department of Agriculture,
dated 4 December 1959

## EFTA

NOTES FOR MEMORANDUM ON POINTS RAISED
IN MR. Ó MUIMHNEACHÁIN'S LETTER
OF 27TH NOVEMBER

(1)  This point is dealt with in this Department's recent
memorandum on Agricultural Aspects of Joining the
Seven.[15]

Membership of EFTA would involve our making bilateral
agricultural arrangements with the other members.
Apart from Britain, these countries have little to give us
agriculturally. Any proposed agreement with Britain would
have to be communicated in the first instance to the other
members of EFTA (Article 29 of Convention), who could
hardly be expected to favour agricultural arrangements
between Ireland and Britain which represented a much
better bargain for Ireland than their own bilateral
agricultural arrangements with Britain represented for
them. It would, therefore, be more difficult to get the
specially favourable treatment in the British market which
our close economic relations with Britain demand.

EFTA is a loose arrangement which relies very largely on
freeing of trade to achieve the objectives, mentioned in
Article 2 of the Convention, of promoting in each member
state "a sustained expansion of economic activity, full
employment, increased productivity and the rational use of
resources, financial stability and continuous improvement
in living standards". The Six, on the other hand, recognise
joint responsibility for mutual development and have
supranational authorities, common funds, etc., for
achieving this objective. If Ireland joined EFTA as an
ordinary member, we would be in danger of losing the
strong bargaining position which we possess in the shape

---

15  Not printed

of our special position (common language and financial institutions, free movement of money and labour, etc.) vis á vis Britain which, on a population basis represents about 60% of the EFTA.

(2) Joining EFTA would expose our industry to greater competition than would our association with Britain alone in a Free Trade Area Arrangement. One could argue, therefore, that we would be justified in looking for greater agricultural concessions (from Britain mainly) as a price for joining EFTA than we would be prepared to accept in a partnership with Britain. This, however, would be almost impossible to achieve in practice.

Should it be eventually decided, for general policy reasons, to enter EFTA, the following would, from a realistic point of view, represent about the most we could bargain for from Britain with any prospect of success:

(a) Abolition of guaranteed price differential and "waiting period", for store cattle and sheep, and, consequently –

(b) application of British guaranteed prices to our fat cattle and carcase meat;

(c) application of British guaranteed prices to our live pigs and/or pork;

(d) an assurance of admission of our agricultural products without quantitative restriction (but we would still be subject to Article 17 of the Convention);

(e) regular discussions between the two Governments on agricultural questions of mutual interest.

(3) Our recent memorandum on agricultural aspects of joining the Seven attempted to show that our interest can best be served by seeking a Free Trade Area arrangement with Britain alone. The main reason is that what we want is Britain's to give, and that joining EFTA would bring little but extra competition in our industrial market.

An economic association with Britain would mean that we would be no longer in *isolation*. We could enter EFTA in due course when we had consolidated our position in the British market and our economy had become sufficiently strong to take on the extra competition; we might, in the meantime, have evolved from a Free Trade Area to a "Common Market" arrangement with Britain, which would enable us to preserve our special relations with Britain even as a member of EFTA.

An attraction for this country in the original Free Trade Area project was the prospect of substantial derogations from the obligations in regard to tariff reductions and quota enlargements while at the same time we could aspire to become a base for new industries which from the beginning would have unrestricted access to the British market and, in addition, preferential access and ultimately full access to the Continental market. As the original concept of a European Free Trade Area has apparently been discarded by the Six (who now apparently want to move, not on a European but on a worldwide or GATT basis) this attraction no longer exists and there seems to be no alternative but to look mainly to Britain for our markets and, to a large extent also, for technical and Capital Assistance in our industrialisation. It is, of course, true that everything depends on Britain also seeing the long-term advantages of such a new arrangement; and the British attitude will be affected by political as well as economic considerations.

The Six see the future as being dominated largely by a few powerful states and groups, e.g. the United States, the Six and Britain, which would share responsibility for, and co-ordinate their efforts to help, the less developed countries. The Six have indicated their willingness to help Greece and Turkey, in addition of course to their own overseas territories. They have gone so far as to question Britain's real interest in helping the less developed countries. From that point of view alone it may suit Britain quite well (in order to minimise demands on her from other sources) to accept some degree of economic "responsibility" for Ireland, e.g. by affording us special commodity arrangements and industrial derogations. Such derogations could be arranged much more simply in a British-Irish Free Trade Area or Common Market than in a wider Free Trade Area.

It would likewise be easier to give Britain permanently a special position in our market in a Free Trade Area or similar arrangement between the two countries, in return for the agricultural benefits and industrial derogations we seek.

It is difficult to see why Britain should want this country to join the EFTA, unless for the purpose of side tracking the proposals we have made to her. Britain alone would have to pay the cost of our admission in the form of an agricultural agreement. She would also be bringing additional competition for her exporters into a market where at present they are predominant.

(4) So far as this Department can see, a Free Trade Area (interim agreement) between Britain and Ireland would not conflict with GATT as the bulk of the trade between the two countries would be covered. Neither would it appear to conflict with Britain's legal obligations to the Commonwealth. The Anglo Australian meat agreement is a precedent for commodity arrangements, of the type we would like to have with Britain. There would however be strong reactions from New Zealand and Australia if we got special terms for milk products and lamb in Britain, but eggs and bacon would not be of much interest to the Commonwealth except possibly bacon in the case of Canada. It should be remembered that Britain would have far better economic advantages in our market in a two country Free Trade Area arrangement than she has in the Commonwealth. Our policy should be to convince the British Government that the new economic relationships between the two countries will be much closer than Britain's trade links with the Commonwealth.

Leabharlanna Fhine Gall

## J.C.B. MacCarthy to C.C. Cremin,[16] 4 December 1959

Dear Cremin

In connection with our recent meeting with the Taoiseach you prepared a list of instances in which there was an indication from the British side that they might wish us to join E.F.T.A. There was some speculation at the meeting as to why the British might wish us to join and a number of possible reasons were mentioned.

We have since been giving some thought to the matter here and we have come to the conclusion that the following may be among the British motives, viz.

(a)  the British would undoubtedly prefer total free entry here to their present preferential conditions;

(b)  they could hardly hope to get this on a bilateral deal but they would ultimately get it if we joined E.F.T.A.;

(c)  if we were in E.F.T.A. the British would probably be better able to get the agreement of the other members to our being given some agricultural concessions, as they could quote to the other members the fact that the latter would be benefiting through free entry to this market;

(d)  on the other hand, they could restrain us from looking for too much in the agricultural sphere by pointing out that they could not give us too much at the expense of other co-members of E.F.T.A. and they could, no doubt, rely on the latter to do the fighting for them in this regard.

We may be unfair in attributing these motives to the British but we nevertheless feel that all concerned should bear in mind the possibility that they do exist.

I am sending copies of this letter to Ó Muimhneacháin, Whitaker, Nagle and O'Brien.

Yours sincerely,
J.C.B. MacCARTHY

---

16 Cornelius "Con" Cremin (1908–87), Secretary, Department of External Affairs (1958–63), later Ambassador to the United Nations (1964–74)

*Memorandum issued from the Department of Finance,
dated 14 December 1959*

## REASONS FOR REDUCING PROTECTION

1.  The inadequacy of a policy of protection as a remedy for the problems of unemployment and emigration has become obvious in recent years with the increasing saturation of the limited home market. The average number engaged in manufacturing industry increased by only 2,000 between 1951 and 1958. It is only through enlarging its sales on export markets that Irish industry can in future provide jobs in increasing numbers for those seeking a livelihood in Ireland. Moreover, a steady increase in exports will be needed to support the greater internal activity and the higher expenditure on imports which will go with a general improvement in employment and living standards.

2.  External purchasers will not turn increasingly towards Irish products unless these products are fully competitive in price and quality. At present this test is satisfied by only a limited range of Irish industrial products. Most of the other countries of Europe have already large and efficient industrial sectors, whose progress is faster than ours. Over the period 1949 to 1958 the volume of our industrial output went up by only 23% whereas in O.E.E.C. countries taken as a whole the increase was 73%. We cannot hope to share in the economic advance of Europe if we merely try to safeguard our industrial status quo. A determined drive for increased efficiency and lower unit costs is obviously essential to enlarge, against ever-increasing competition, our sales in export markets.

3.  The non-competitiveness of many of our industrial products is related to the smallness of the home market, the inadequate utilisation of productive capacity and the lack of opportunities for economies of scale and specialisation. The only remedy for these deficiencies is to bring about

[51]

an expansion of effective demand for the products of Irish industry. This can be done in two ways:

(1) by attracting external purchasers through the offer of high quality goods at competitive prices; and

(2) by raising real incomes and purchasing power in the non-industrial sector of the economy, as is the aim of our policy in relation to agricultural exports and tourism.

Progress under (1) depends primarily on raising productivity but it would be greatly helped by success under (2). An increase in effective demand, resulting in longer "runs" and fuller utilisation of capacity, would reduce unit costs of production and help to bring prices down to international levels, thus widening the market for Irish products.

4.  The urgency of action to bring down the cost and improve the quality of our manufactures is made all the greater by the emergence of the Six and the Seven. Competition in export markets will grow according as the major countries of Europe, through tariff reductions and freer trade, achieve greater specialisation, higher output and lower costs.

5.  High protective tariffs are associated with and reinforce the non-competitiveness of Irish manufactures. In the case of the vast bulk of our protected industries exports form only a small proportion of output. The scale of protection is such that in many industries there is no effective competition at present. There are over 400 protective tariff references and of these over 100 provide for tariffs of more than 50% ad valorem (full) or $33\frac{1}{3}\%$ (preferential). A gradually increasing element of competition on the home market would be a much more general and effective spur to improvements in efficiency than special aids and incentives to which only the progressive undertakings will respond. As long as high protection is maintained there will be no compulsion to get into shape for export markets. Sheltered

against the normal consequences of inertia, unprogressive managements can use the high protection they enjoy to make inefficiency profitable.

6.  High protection provides too much scope for mutually beneficial arrangements between employers and workers to the detriment of the consumer and the national interest. Cost increases in protected industries, arising out of excessive profits and wages, are transmitted to other industries and reduce their efficiency and competitiveness. There is a real danger that, if there continues to be no discipline of tariff reduction here, despite the growth of free trade elsewhere, industries now able to export economically will be reduced to a non-competitive status.

7.  A particular case of this cost-transmission is where materials are protected and their higher price adds to the cost of producing finished goods for export. It has been represented, for example, that manufacturers of upholstered furniture would not be able to compete with Six-County manufacturers in the Twenty-Six County market because the cost of upholstery materials manufactured here is not competitive. In fact, protection creates a vicious circle, since users of protected high-priced products must in turn seek protection in some form. They try to make up for the higher cost of their purchases by demanding higher prices for their products or higher rewards for their services. In the end, protection leads not only to transfers of income within the community but also to a general rise in the cost structure of the economy. High costs of production are reflected in high prices which reduce the real value of incomes. The consequent lowering of living standards vis-à-vis Britain heightens the "demonstration effect" and tends to encourage emigration.

8.  One of the arguments advanced for protection of Irish products – and it amounts almost to an argument for *permanent* protection no matter how good or cheap they are – is that even the efficient Irish manufacturer could not make headway in an unprotected home market against

the expensively-advertised and strongly-established brands of foreign competitors. There is less force in this point, however, if protection is only gradually lowered, and particularly if this is done in the context of an agricultural exports arrangement which increases purchasing power on the home market. Irish manufacturers able to expand exports on the basis of competitiveness in price and quality should at least be able to hold their own in a larger home market. The reputation of their products would be enhanced by their success in the export field. No suggestion of inferiority attaches at present to Irish-produced stout, whiskey, biscuits, cut glass, ropes, etc.; and the list would lengthen according as capacity to sell abroad was established.

9. Over the past eighteen months or so, a number of our more enterprising manufacturers have succeeded in expanding their sales abroad. In fact, the rise in industrial production over the past year has been based largely on export sales. It has been contended that some protected industries maintain an export trade by charging all overheads against home sales and that, in such cases, the capacity to export would be hampered if foreign competition had to be met on the home market. The capacity of such industries to enlarge their export sales will, however, remain limited and precarious unless and until their productivity is improved; and this will not occur as a consequence of maintaining protection but rather as a consequence of their having to meet increased competition on the home market.

10. Tariffs are justifiable economically only as a *temporary* help for "infant industries" or "young economies" to realise long-run comparative advantages. The case for freer trade rests on the increased productivity made possible by international specialisation in accordance with comparative advantages. A growing number of countries are now formally recognising, by their participation in Common Markets, Free Trade Areas, G.A.T.T., etc., the mutual benefits to be derived from freer trade. It is realised that one country does not gain at the expense of another;

all gain by reason of the general increase in production secured. It would be difficult otherwise to understand the participation in free trade arrangements of countries differing considerably in resources, population, income, and degree of industrialisation.

11. The risk of exposure to competition from larger units is often exaggerated. In many industries the smaller scale firm may be the more efficient. There are, for example, no mass production factories in Switzerland. One-third of Switzerland's total production is exported and most of these exports are industrial products although almost all the raw materials have to be imported. In many cases virtually the whole value of the product represents the value added by Swiss labour and technical competence. Efficiency, good management, drive and capacity for hard work have enabled Switzerland, a small country endowed with few of the natural advantages enjoyed by her larger neighbours, to compete successfully in world markets. In a wide market there would be a better chance for our medium and small enterprises to specialise, for example, in distinctive fashion goods.

12. A gradual but steady reduction of protection over a period of years would ensure more intense concentration by management and workers on the raising of efficiency and productivity and reinforce the fiscal and other incentives to increase production for export. The pace of technical development may be expected to quicken in the outside world. Some driving force is needed to bring our production and marketing methods up to competitive pitch and to keep them there.

13. In a climate of expanding demand for Irish exports and increasing internal activity and development, there would be less resistance to the introduction of labour-saving equipment and devices and to the closing down of industries unable ever to adapt themselves to competitive conditions.

14. As far back as 1947 the Department of Industry and Commerce recognised the need for some discipline to increase industrial efficiency. In that year legislation was prepared and approved by the Government providing wide powers for continuous supervision of the efficiency of manufacturing businesses and, if necessary, for formal inquiries into the efficiency of such businesses. It was felt that there was a necessity to ensure reasonable standards of efficiency in industries which enjoyed the benefits of tariff or quota restrictions on imports. It would appear to be much preferable that the discipline necessary to secure a general increase in industrial efficiency should be applied by gradual exposure to external competition rather than by internal administrative measures.

15. Opposition to the lowering of tariffs may stem as much from what the French call "immobilisme" as from a genuine fear of business failure or unemployment. Some of the weaker firms would, of course, be endangered but increased efficiency and competitiveness would result from the pressure towards amalgamation and specialisation exerted by a régime of tariff reduction. The risk of unemployment tends to be assessed without regard to the adaptive power of industry over the transition period. The need to look to expanding export industries for an enduring increase in employment may, on the other hand, be forgotten. Only the less efficient industries would be hurt by the gradual lowering of tariffs. The current high level of industrial production which shows no signs of slackening would make the present an appropriate time to begin to lower tariffs.

16. In a recent pamphlet entitled "European Free Trade and the Prospects for Irish Industry" the National Council of the Federation of Irish Industries recognises that fundamental changes in economic policies are imminent and will involve progressive reduction of protection for Irish industries leading eventually to free trade conditions. The Council believes that Irish industry is sufficiently strong and adaptable not only to meet the situation but

also to develop and prosper "provided that action is taken in time by individual firms and by industries and that the co-operation and assistance of the Government is forthcoming". It is an encouraging sign that the Council's reaction to the current trend towards freer trade is one of confidence. In the transition period, while the sheltering screen of protection is being gradually lowered, State aid, in the form of loan capital on reasonable terms, technical assistance grants, etc., could be made available to assist in the process of adaptation and modernisation of industry. The Federation of Irish Industries might in due course be asked for any specific proposals they may wish to make in this regard.

17. It has been shown above that a progressive lowering of tariffs is necessary for our economic progress, whatever may be happening in the outside world. It is all the more necessary in view of the current movement in Europe towards freer trade and the increased competition to which this will give rise. The advantage of participation in some form of free trade arrangement is that it will secure some payment or return for what it would be advantageous for us to do of our own accord. It will enable us to share more certainly in the economic advance of countries more favoured than ours. A closer degree of association with the international economy, through reduced protection and participation in a free trade arrangement, would help to compensate for the narrowness of the domestic market, more especially if it also promised a surer and better market for agricultural exports. It is only by gearing ourselves for a growing trade with the rest of the world that we can tackle, with real prospect of success, the problems of unemployment and emigration.

## T.K. Whitaker to J.C. Nagle,[17] 16 December 1959

Dear Nagle,
It was agreed, when the "four Secretaries" last met, that we would, inter alia, look at your "Notes for Memorandum on points raised in Mr. Ó Muimhneacháin's letter of 27th November" to see if we had any comments to offer.

On Point (1) of that letter we in Finance sent our detailed comments to Industry and Commerce on 4 December, followed on 14 December by a special memorandum entitled "Reasons for Reducing Protection". I have sent you copies of both documents.

I agree with your general thesis that there would probably be greater advantage for us in a "free trade" arrangement with Britain alone than in joining EFTA. At the same time, I think too much could be made of our "strong bargaining position" vis-à-vis Britain. The various ties mentioned (common language and financial system, free movement of money and labour, etc.) do not add to – indeed, may subtract from – our bargaining power, which, in the last resort, is to be measured by our capacity to deny the British our custom, without hurting ourselves. On this definition, I doubt if we have much bargaining power anywhere in the world.

I suggest also that it may be too extreme to say that "joining EFTA would bring little but extra competition in our industrial market". This is no doubt intended to refer only to the industrial aspects but, even so, it seems to overlook the increased openings for industrial exports which membership of EFTA would provide and the desirability, in our own interest, of accepting gradually increasing competition in the home market by a lowering of protective tariffs.

---

17 John Charles ('Jack') Nagle (1910–96), Secretary, Department of Agriculture, later Chairman of the National Council for Educational Awards.

On the question of our being a base for new export industries, it is said that the attraction of our having "unrestricted access to the British market and, in addition, preferential access and ultimately full access to the Continental market" no longer exists. While preferential access to the markets of the Six would not be available until a nexus was established between the Six and the Seven, Ireland, as a member of EFTA, would provide preferential access not only to Britain, as at present, but also to the other countries of EFTA, who are by no means negligible importers.

As to why Britain might want us to join EFTA, MacCarthy, in his letter of 4 December to Cremin, may have appraised the situation fairly closely. It is possible that what the British feel able to concede on the agricultural side (and to accept on the industrial) would not go far enough in their view to justify a distinctive "free trade" arrangement between the two countries. This, of course, is not a reason for our refraining from pressing them hard for special, bilateral terms.

I agree with the stress you lay on the points (1) that what we want is Britain's to give, (2) that isolation is to be avoided and (3) that a satisfactory arrangement with Britain, while best calculated to help us immediately, would also provide a basis for further development of economic relations with Britain herself and for liaison with EFTA, and such wider groupings as may in future emerge.

Yours sincerely,
T.K. WHITAKER

c.c. Mr. Ó Muimhneacháin
    Mr. Cremin
    Mr. MacCarthy

*C.C. Cremin to T.K. Whitaker with general observations on*
*"Reasons for Reducing Protection" attached, 21 December 1959*

Confidential

Dear Whitaker,
You sent me on 14th December copy of your Memorandum
"Reasons for Reducing Protection" which you forwarded to
MacCarthy on that date.

I enclose a note containing a general observation on
that document. This observation is, in many ways, rather
platitudinous, will certainly be present to your mind and has,
I am sure, often been made before – it has, in any case, often
been made in submissions to the OEEC over the last 10 years.
However, on the principle that *cela va sans dire mais cela va*
*mieux en le disant,* I thought it best to make it again, especially
as I have always felt personally that the factor in question does
affect in a really vital fashion economic development here.

Yours sincerely,
C.C. CREMIN

c.c.: J.C.B. MacCarthy
J.C. Nagle
M. Ó Muimhneacháin

CONFIDENTIAL

DEPARTMENT OF FINANCE MEMORANDUM
OF 14th DECEMBER, 1959
ON REASONS FOR REDUCING PROTECTION

1. While not all the arguments adduced in favour of the thesis urged in the Department of Finance Memorandum "Reasons for Reducing Protection" are necessarily valid (vide par. 6), a good case appears to be made for modifying our protection policy and for bringing to bear an international commitment. It is a question, however, whether there is not a tendency to discount, on the basis of abstract reasoning which may not be entirely applicable in practice, the possible adverse effects of the removal of protection.

2. It could be contended that, in the economic field, the circumstances prevailing in this country are in some ways so unusual as to weaken, or at least introduce serious qualifications to, otherwise sound theoretical conclusions even when they can be supported by experience elsewhere.

3. The point has frequently been made in many of the documents produced over the past nine months in the course of the study of closer economic association with Britain that we have, in effect, an economic union with that country in the matter of free movement of currency and manpower. These two phenomena, and particularly the second, could, however, constitute a serious impediment to the development here of the same kind of reaction as might occur elsewhere to a particular set of measures. Not only is there free movement of manpower between this country and Britain, but there is also the very important fact that Irishmen and women have a most remarkable "mobility" by reference both to inclination and to their admissibility to other countries (including Britain). This is perhaps, indeed, the most striking feature which differentiates our population and emigration situation from that of other countries confronted with problems in this particular field.

Whereas, for instance, an essential aspect of our problem is to bring about an increase in population (more jobs being a means to that end). The Italian problem, for instance, is that of finding outlets for surplus population. Our objective is, however, impeded by the extraordinary freedom with which our people are prepared to, and can, go abroad, whereas Italy's problem is complicated by, and to some extent arises from, the inability of her people to secure admission elsewhere.

4. If more of our people stayed at home or were unable to go abroad, their very presence, engendering greater competition and inventiveness, would lead to an increase in the gross national product through the urge to maintain and increase the present standard of living. One has the impression that something like this has happened in Holland, which was confronted in the early post-war years with the prospect of a disquietingly large increase in population coupled with a loss of overseas earnings and outlets for emigration, but where the problem seems to have been largely solved through greater effort in all fields of economic activity.

5. As long as the existing freedom of outward movement prevails, the possibility exists that a setback in industrial production for whatever cause (including the reduction and removal of protection) will result not in higher productivity and greater competitiveness but in an outflow of redundant manpower.

6. A general qualification to the argumentation in the Memorandum is that it rather discounts the fact that we have had for many years past at our doorstep a substantial free-entry market in Britain – a market which represents approximately 60% of EFTA. In detail there is somewhat of a contradiction between the observations in paragraph 3 of the Memorandum and those in paragraph 11, the internal Swiss market not being so markedly greater than our own. One might wonder, too, whether it is realistic to adduce the case of Switzerland as a good parallel for this country: it is

doubtful whether we can expect to find widely prevalent in Ireland for a very long time to come those individual qualities which are such a characteristic of the Swiss and which have been largely responsible for their marked material success.

### T.K. Whitaker to C.C. Cremin, 22 December 1959

Confidential

Dear Cremin,
Thanks for your note of 21st December on our memorandum
"Reasons for Reducing Protection".

I was somewhat doubtful about including the reference
to Switzerland although I thought it apt enough. I always
feel it is wiser to avoid drawing parallels between different
countries. They are too easy to contest and the discounting of
any particular point by an opponent seems to weaken one's
general argument. I do not think, however, that the validity of
the thesis in our memorandum depends in the slightest on the
appositeness of the reference to Switzerland.

Nor do I think the force of our reasoning is lessened by
describing it as "abstract" or by referring to our conclusions as
"theoretical". I have yet to see any convincing argument, on
practical or theoretical grounds, for the opposite thesis, i.e.
that the maintenance of a policy of high protection will raise
employment and living standards and reduce emigration.

Your main point, however, is that the exceptional (outward)
mobility of Irish men and women poses a special problem.
This is, of course, a factor that no one considering our
development prospects can afford to neglect. It was very
present to my mind when writing the opening chapter of
"Economic Development"; indeed, I may say it set the tone
of the whole study, in which constant stress is laid on the
disposition to emigrate and on the crucial importance, in
consequence, of the *acceptability* of domestic living standards.

But it is unjustifiable to proceed from a recognition of this
factor to the conclusion that emigration would be accentuated
by reducing protection. I believe that the *opposite* conclusion

is the more tenable for reasons which are developed in our memorandum but were summarised as follows in paragraph 5 of Chapter 1 of "Economic Development":–

> "The possibility of freer trade in Europe carries disquieting implications for some Irish industries and raises special problems of adaptation and adjustment. It necessitates also a re-appraisal of future industrial and agricultural prospects. It seems clear that, sooner or later, protection will have to go and the challenge of free trade be accepted. There is really no other choice for a country wishing to keep pace materially with the rest of Europe. It would be a policy of despair to accept that our costs of production must permanently be higher than those of other European countries, either in industry or in agriculture. Our level of real incomes depends on our competitive efficiency. If that must be lower than in the rest of Europe we should have to be content with relatively low living standards. With the alternative of emigration available we are unlikely, either as a community or as individuals, to accept such a situation for long unless it is seen as an essential part of a programme of national regeneration. The effect of any policy entailing relatively low living standards here for all time would be to sustain and stimulate the outflow of emigrants and in the end jeopardise our economic independence. Any little benefit obtained in terms of employment in protected non-competitive industries would be outweighed by losses through emigration and general economic impoverishment. If we do not expand production on a competitive basis, we shall fail to provide the basis necessary for the economic independence and material progress of the community."

You postulate in paragraph 5 of your note a setback in industrial production as a result of the reduction of protection and a consequential "outflow of redundant manpower". One must interpret this as meaning a net (or overall) fall in industrial output and employment, not just a check or fall in this industry or that, which might be counterbalanced by increases in others. You give no grounds for making such an extreme assumption. Even if it were true – and I do not think it is – would it be an argument for being satisfied with the status quo? I have given in the memorandum and in the passage just quoted from "Economic Development" what I regard as sound reasons for the view that continuance of a high protection policy offers no prospect of increased industrial output and employment; rather does it promise a virtually uncurbed flow of emigration.

It is not right to claim, as you do in paragraph 6, that the argumentation in our memorandum "discounts the fact that we have had for many years past at our doorstep a substantial free entry market in Britain – a market which represents approximately 60% of EFTA". The burden of our case is that this export market has not been properly exploited because high protection has been accompanied by relatively high costs which, over a wide field, make exports non-competitive while it has, at the same time, induced contentment with the limited but profitable home market.

I am very pleased to see you record your agreement that there is a good case for modifying our protection policy and for bringing to bear an international commitment. Like you, I would be greatly opposed to any over-hasty action which would prejudice the future development of our industries. But I strongly suggest that we can be over-timid about the scaling down of protection having regard to the urgent and vital need to increase our competitiveness in the export field. In considering the "possible adverse effects" of removal of protection, let us not forget the undoubtedly adverse consequences of being left stranded on a high and narrow protectionist plateau on which acceptable living standards could be provided only temporarily and for a diminishing number of our people.

I have made my points rather vigorously in this note but I am sure you will not mind since our joint aim is to reach the right conclusion and this can best be achieved by the cut and thrust of argument.

Yours sincerely,
T.K. WHITAKER

c.c.: M. Ó Muimhneacháin
J.C.B. MacCarthy
J.C. Nagle

## J.C.B. MacCarthy to T.K. Whitaker, 22 December 1959

Dear Whitaker,

Many thanks for your letter of the 14th December and the memorandum setting out the case for reducing protection, as your Department sees it.

I have refrained from sending notes to you, Nagle or Cremin concerning the various memoranda which you have respectively sent to me for the purposes of the study requested by the Taoiseach, as outlined in Ó Muimhneacháin's letter of the 27th November. I did so because it was agreed that the Department of Industry and Commerce would prepare a composite memorandum on the implications of joining EFTA which would incorporate the views of all Departments. This memo, as you know, is well in hands, though we still await the information which the Central Statistics Office was to prepare.

I feel, however, that I ought to say at this stage in relation to your memorandum on the desirability of reducing protection that I cannot accept the views set out in it other than as a, if you will not mind my putting it that way, somewhat idealistic approach which is not, as I am sure you will agree, backed by anything more than faith in the operation of the economic laws which are expounded.

In this Department, however, we have had a great deal of experience of the sensitivity of our industries to shifts or reductions in demand and we have had many unhappy experiences of the way in which unemployment situations can pile up almost overnight because of factors which in themselves might not appear to be of enormous moment. The harsh realities of the situation are that we have our industries, with many thousands of people employed in them, and we cannot really afford to use them as guinea-pigs. I think the fact that your Department agreed, even as recently as a couple of months ago, to our spending State funds on propaganda in favour of the purchase of Irish goods is one of the best answers

[68]

I could give to your Department's challenge of our view that public prejudice would operate in favour of imported goods if the tariff barriers were lowered. Add to this consideration the fact that large-scale manufacturers in Britain could send enough material in here in next to no time to swamp the market in any particular line for a fairly long period ahead and you have a measure of the risk to which we should be exposing our industries. You say protection is only for "infant" industries but ours are not yet out of their teens and still need a measure of parentalism. It is well to remember that if the war years and their immediate aftermath are excluded, as they ought to be, our industries have not had much more than a decade of protection. Even the adult industries of the great industrial nations need and get protection.

I think there is a danger of being led, perhaps involuntarily, from your advocacy of the discipline of tariff reductions to advocacy of complete free trade. This is an easy transition to make in the abstract but they are two entirely different things in practice. While we could conceive of industries being subjected to well thought out and prudent cuts in protection as an incentive to efficiency, these cuts would have to be made very carefully and on a basis that would not leave us without the power speedily to reverse engines as and when experience dictated.

I do not wish to anticipate the views which we will express in the draft of the comprehensive memorandum but I thought it well to send you this note so that you may have a chance, before we meet again, of tempering economic theory to the facts of our industrial life. I have assumed, I hope rightly, that your memorandum was intended to be provocative rather than doctrinaire.

Yours sincerely,
J.C.B. MacCARTHY

Dear MacCarthy,
Before we enter the season of goodwill I feel I should make a short comment on your letter of 22nd December, which rather unfairly tries to force me into accepting, as applying to our memorandum "Reasons for Reducing Protection", either of two denigratory epithets, "provocative" or "doctrinaire". I hope that on reconsideration you will treat this reasoned document not as putting forward an "idealistic" approach but – for reasons given in it and elaborated in the letter I sent Cremin yesterday – as containing, in my view, the essence of realism.

The title of the memorandum was carefully chosen and the argument is not pushed to the point of advocacy of complete free trade – certainly not as an immediate or early prospect. It advocates rather a progressive discipline of tariff reductions with the right (as we would have even on Portuguese terms) to arrest the process where any major industry came under dangerous stress.

We both of us know people who are more Catholic than the Pope; should Industry and Commerce not guard against being more protectionist than the Federation of Irish Industries?

I would ask you to ponder the point of view set out in my letter yesterday to Cremin. I am personally convinced that the issue is not one of economic theory but one that bears directly on our hopes of further development.

With that, I wish you all the best for Christmas and the New Year!

Yours sincerely,
T.K. WHITAKER

c.c. Mr. Ó Muimhneacháin, Mr. Cremin, Mr. Nagle

## M.D. McCarthy[18] to T.K. Whitaker, 24 December 1959

Dear Whitaker,

I had jotted down some of these general remarks, but was very doubtful about sending them to you since I did not think that they could contribute much to the argument about the problem of industrial development and the desirability of promoting efficiency by tariff reduction etc., whether forced to adherence to one of the European communities or otherwise. There is nothing novel in what follows, but, in the light of our recent conversation, some of the remarks seem relevant, and I am sending them to you even though they may not be adapted in their present form for general circulation.

It is obvious from what you have written that you fully recognise that a very important pre-condition for a change in policy is an alteration in the outlook of those who are charged with facilitating or inducing industrial development. I believe that many of the people concerned do not fully recognise yet, what is clearly set out in the Memorandum of 8th July, 1959,[19] that any future expansion in industry here is completely dependent on attracting external demand for its products and that this involves reduction in unit costs and an improvement in quality of the goods and in productivity. Or, if they accept this proposition they do not realise its implications and in particular the inconsistency between it and the aim of supplying a small home market, which at best can expand only slowly, with a full range of consumer goods. It is, of course, not true to say that industry was fostered here without any advertance to the cost of the consumer, but it is probably true to say that employment was the main aim and cost was only secondary. Now this has to change since we cannot get out of the present situation unless we can break into export markets and this involves a change of emphasis, putting cost first. The increase in employment is not being disregarded but it

18 Director, Central Statistics Office and later President of University College, Cork
19 Not printed

[71]

must be recognised that it can be achieved only if an efficient production can be built up.

This will involve inevitably a greater emphasis of specialisation on certain industries and also some willingness to recognise the advantages of relying to some extent on the international division of labour. We must be ready to import some consumer goods that we cannot efficiently produce here, if we are to expect other countries to take those which we can sell. Nobody suggests that we should sacrifice an existing industry merely to make it possible for the foreigners to sell here what we cannot develop and at the same time freeze the present industrial set up. We must be prepared to scrap as well as build if we are to grow. It is obviously difficult to get this change in outlook across in an economy obsessed with the presence (or continued departure) of unemployed resources but it is clear that some sort of specialisation will have to develop in industry here. It must be recognised too that progress involves getting out of unprofitable lines as well as into profitable ones, and the test of "profitability" in this connection is the ability to sell in export markets.

It seems to me too, that while exhortations and measures which attempt to increase exports generally are probably useful, there will need to be some selectivity exercised in this field as in others. We appear to be acting in contradiction to the well known military principle of concentration of resources, and dissipating our energies on a very wide range. It is difficult in a free economy for a central body to make a selection and perhaps all that can be done at the moment is to help everybody interested, and to concentrate on the more profitable lines later. But even if we select certain lines on which to push exports we should not concentrate all our energies on marketing alone. There are very often technical, manufacturing or legal problems involved, such as the measures which may be needed to ensure that the bacterial count of milk is low enough to make it possible to manufacture cheese properly and investigation of the type of cheese best suited to our conditions. The whole field of both production and marketing needs to be tackled together in such sectors.

There is one further point that should be made and that is the desirability from the development point of view of getting increased profits into the corporate sector and particularly into the industrial part of it. This is important from two points of view. In the first place it will tend to increase savings, for while perhaps, say, 5 per cent of personal income is saved the proportion in the case of corporations is probably of the order of 50 per cent. In the second place the availability of corporate savings in industry will mean that investment in productive enterprise is stimulated, partly because the money will be in the hands of those most likely to make productive investment and partly because if the enterprise is already profitable then there will be an inducement to expand. Hitherto, in the protectionist economy, the public naturally had strong feelings against big profits. If, however, industry produces at a level of costs which is competitive with imports then the feeling against the increase in profits cannot be so strong, particularly if they are earned on exports. This seems to me an important point and one worth taking some risks to achieve. The best way to lower costs would be to face the industrialists with the certainty that tariffs are going to come down and in their present mood I feel that they will accept this pressure and react favourably to it. One further small point is that there is probably a great deal of unused capacity in Irish industry. Lowering of costs will make it profitable to use such capacity for exports and the increase in output will probably be much greater than that generated by new investment.

Yours sincerely,
M.D. McCARTHY

Dear Whitaker,
I received your letter of the 16th December about the points
raised in Ó Muimhneacháin's letter of the 27th November and
am glad to note that there is a large measure of agreement
between us. On the points you mention, I am sending you
the following comments by way of explanation of our point of
view.

Our original theory on close economic relations with Britain
was on the lines of that put forward by Professor Carter to the
effect that at present we are getting the worst of both worlds;
important factors of production, i.e. labour and capital,
move freely out of the country, while the counterpart of this,
i.e. unified prices and markets and joint responsibility for
development, are lacking. Professor Carter's advice was that
we should either make the economies more separate, which
would be very difficult, or move closer to get the benefits
which our farmers need in the way of equivalent prices, etc.
If the British do not prove susceptible to closer relations, then
another alternative to joining the Seven might have to be
considered. As Professor Carter states, it would, undoubtedly,
be extremely difficult to make the economies more separate,
but the existence of the Common Market, with its guaranteed
markets and prices for agriculture and its acceptance of joint
responsibility for development, makes the proposal at least
a possible runner. Britain would hardly care to contemplate
the possibility of Ireland being forced into the arms of the
Common Market, or even being forced to negotiate an
agreement for association with that body. However unrealistic
this second alternative may be, it would be no harm if we
could convey to the British that –

(a)  we are not prepared to remain as we are, "enjoying" the
worst of both worlds;

(b)  if they are not prepared to make an appropriate
settlement, taking account of the significance for our

economy of the factors referred to by us (i.e. common language and financial system, etc.), then they may be forcing us to consider some form of association with the Common Market as an alternative – indeed, there is a body of opinion in this country which feels that this might be a good thing in the long run.

It is for these reasons that we feel that the elements of our close association should be thoroughly underlined and understood on all sides rather than that we should weaken our case by a tendency to ignore their existence and importance. If our case for special agricultural treatment (superior to New Zealand and Denmark) does not rest on these elements, on what else can it rest, and how can Britain justify "a distinctive free trade arrangement" with Ireland on any other grounds? If there is any doubt about these matters, then the sooner they are resolved the better. In fact, at an early stage in this exercise, when Departments were asked to submit lists of questions to be examined by an inter-departmental committee, our very first suggestion was that Professor Carter's theory and the implications for our future development of the existence of a "virtual common market in manpower and capital" with Britain, as well as the applicability of Common Market principles and concepts, should be looked into.

As one of Britain's best customers in Europe, we should in reality have as much bargaining power as any other country, and, in addition, there is scope for the diversion to Britain of millions of pounds worth of custom now going elsewhere.

Our statement that "joining EFTA would bring little but extra competition in our industrial market" is, of course, based on our own estimate of the openings likely to exist for agricultural exports in the other six, and the view expressed by the Department of Industry and Commerce that "the prospects of increasing exports to those countries . . . are not encouraging". Industry and Commerce are very conscious of the fact that they already have free access to the industrial market of Britain and that, in return for the "disadvantages" of extra competition which membership of EFTA would bring, they would be getting access to an additional market of only 35,000,000 people – granted, as you say, that these have a high purchasing power. Our original Free Trade Area thinking was probably conditioned mainly by the prospects of additional openings in the 160,000,000 market of the Six. However, I quite agree that there would be some extra openings in EFTA and that increased competition would tend to make for more efficient industries. At the same time, I sometimes wonder if competition alone would do the trick and whether an effective programme of industrialisation genuinely backed by large-scale British and American industry is not equally essential. (Such a programme would be dependent on our arrival at overall satisfactory understandings with Britain.) In an open economy with Britain, the first reaction of a manufacturer to competition might be to let workers go (to Britain) to be followed by the flight of capital. In other words, the whole question of the implications of the lack of a separate labour market raised in O'Mahony's article in the Summer, 1959, issue of Studies needs to be looked into in the context of any British/Irish understanding.

I would hesitate to accept the view put forward in MacCarthy's letter of the 4th December to Cremin as to why Britain might want us to join EFTA. Personally, I do not think we have any real information as yet on British thinking on this subject. True, there have been certain casual remarks. When the original Free Trade Area proposal emerged, Britain apparently took the view (as did some international commentators) that there was little in this to attract Ireland. Britain was taken aback to find that such a suggestion was received with chagrin in Ireland and that we were, in fact, keen on joining – if we got suitable terms. In the circumstances, Britain, I imagine, would be slow now to tell us to keep out of the Seven. All along, she has been particularly careful not to give us the impression that she wants us out. Britain has very real difficulties (in view of her commitments to her farmers and to Denmark) in meeting our demands for certain commodities, principally pigs and eggs. Moreover, it may be, to some extent, embarrassing internationally for Britain to be involved simultaneously in a three tier membership of varying degrees of tightness, i.e. with Ireland, with the Commonwealth and with the Seven. Her membership of the Commonwealth was the obstacle which brought down the original free trade area plan. In certain ways, it would be easier for Britain to justify a kind of Benelux inside the Seven than a third international attachment.

It is for the above reasons that we think it is important to

(a) stress the essential differences in British/Irish connections as compared with those existing between Britain and any other country, and

(b) formalise the arrangements in such a way as to make them easier for Britain to justify internationally.

Yours sincerely,<br>
J.C. NAGLE

## J.C.B. MacCarthy to T.K. Whitaker, 24 December 1959

Dear Ken,

Even nearer the season of goodwill, but sincerely, let me assure you that I did not use the word "provocative" in a denigratory sense. What I sought to convey was that I took your memorandum to be intended to be "inducive", if you will, of thought and, therefore, that you would welcome an equally emphatic statement of any opposing points of view.

We feel it to be our duty here to make the most realistic forecast we can of the likely effects on industrial production; and, of course, in the context of EFTA, we would be working towards complete free trade. Having set out the risks as we see them, it is, of course, a matter for consideration whether the overall economic interests of the country justify incurring those risks. My letter was merely directed towards correcting a tendency, which I honestly believe exists, to under-estimate these risks. I think Cremin made a very valuable point in his letter to you which reinforces our own appreciation of the risks.

I feel that we are likely to make better progress if we face the fact that these risks exist rather than attempt to write them off as alarmist. I am sure you would not wish to be unfair in any comment you might make but I do think the third paragraph of your letter of the 23rd December hits a bit below the belt. After all, it is the Government and not the Federation of Irish Industries, that has to take the decision.

One last comment! You have laid some stress on the point that industrialisation, under protection, has not solved the unemployment problem and that the continuation of the present policy of industrialisation, under protection, will not provide the expansion we require. I am compelled to ask where would we be, so far as employment is concerned, if we had not had the protective policy and, even if it is not a cure for all our ills, is it logical to toss it overboard, unless it is clear that something better can be substituted which will not only maintain the employment at the existing level but give the scope for expansion which is desired! All I am seeking is to get the alternatives clearly stated so that a considered choice can be recommended.

I wish you a very happy Christmas and every success in the New Year – though I expect, and hope, you will have gone home by the time this arrives.

Yours sincerely,
J.C.B. MacCARTHY

## C.C. Cremin to T.K. Whitaker, 29 December 1959

Dear Whitaker,

Many thanks for your letter of 22nd instant concerning your memorandum on the reasons for reducing protection.

Needless to say, I most sincerely hope that the studies in train will give the most fruitful results for the improvement of our economic position and I trust that nothing I have said or written could be held to imply the contrary. I was aware, as I said in my covering letter of 21st December, that the point made in the note enclosed therewith was present to your mind and I appreciate entirely the force of the further considerations you have urged. I thought it just as well, nevertheless, to call attention to something which is not so much a postulate or an assumption as a theoretical possibility (as stated in para. 5 of our note) resting on the phenomenon treated in the earlier paragraphs.

Yours sincerely,
C.C. CREMIN

*T.K. Whitaker to J.C.B. MacCarthy with document entitled
"Summary of Propositions" attached, 31 December 1959*

Dear MacCarthy,

Thanks for your letter of 24 December and your good wishes.

It is my anxiety, as it is yours, that decisions about protection
and membership of free trade groupings will be based on a
full appreciation of all the relevant considerations. I think our
"dialogue" may help to elucidate these considerations and that
it can usefully be carried a stage further even at the risk of
some repetition.

You point to the industrialisation which has been achieved
with the aid of protection and, in the light of your experience
of the sensitivity of Irish industries, emphasise the risks of
industrial setback and unemployment inherent in even a
gradual commitment to dispense with protection. While you
recognise that cuts in protective tariffs can be an incentive
to efficiency, you want to retain the right to decide what
industries should bear these cuts, what the cuts should be and
how they should be timed, and you want the power to reverse
engines at any time.

I for my part do not deny that the establishment and present
stage of development of many of our existing industries would
not have been secured without protection – so much indeed is
positively asserted in paragraph 14 of Chapter 2 of "Economic
Development". Nor do I wish to see understated (any more
than I wish to see overstated) the risks for existing industries
involved in premature withdrawal of protection. I do, however,
think it vital in relation to national development prospects to
emphasise the following points:

(a)  protected manufacture for a home market of present
     population and purchasing power and already well
     exploited offers little prospect of *increased* employment;

(b)  in an increasingly competitive world, in which real

[81]

wages will be rising, continued high protection cannot guarantee the maintenance of existing employment in Ireland at *acceptable* real wages;

(c) if employment opportunities are to be created for the fresh thousands seeking work every year – indeed, even if existing employment is to be safeguarded – industry must quickly become more efficient so that its products can be sold on an increasing scale in export markets; and

(d) the rapid and general increase in industrial efficiency required by national progress can most effectively and advantageously be secured by accepting an external commitment to reduce tariffs accompanied by appropriate internal incentives and aids towards industrial adaptation and modernisation.

These conclusions are substantiated in the recent memorandum "Reasons for Reducing Protection". The main thesis was already outlined in "Economic Development" and I must ask your forbearance if I quote again from paragraph 5 of Chapter 1 of that work, which summarises the result (I have not seen it contested) of long study and observation of our economic situation:

"Our level of real income depends on our competitive efficiency. If that must be lower than in the rest of Europe we should have to be content with relatively low living standards. With the alternative of emigration available we are unlikely, either as a community or as individuals, to accept such a situation for long unless it is seen as an essential part of a programme of national regeneration. The effect of any policy entailing relatively low living standards here for all time would be to sustain and stimulate the outflow of emigrants and in the end jeopardise our economic independence. Any little benefit obtained in terms of employment in protected non-competitive industries would be outweighed by losses through emigration and general economic impoverishment".

You ask in your letter "where would we be so far as
employment is concerned if we had not had the protective
policy and, even if it is not a cure for all our ills, is it logical to
toss it overboard unless it is clear that something better can
be substituted which will not only maintain the employment
at the existing level but give the scope for expansion which is
desired?".

No one is suggesting that the policy of protection be tossed
overboard. Even in EFTA the Portuguese have the right to
impose new protective tariffs up to the 1st July, 1972, and
protection will be abolished only gradually by all members,
with provision for resort to quantitative import restrictions if
an appreciable rise in unemployment results in any particular
sector of industry. We can, if we wish, look for better terms
than Portugal as a condition of participation in any free trade
association but do not let us forget that protection will not
of itself sell our goods. It is only if our goods are produced
efficiently enough to sell abroad that we will be able to expand
our output and employment. It would not be to our own
advantage to slow down unduly the process of adaptation to
competitive world conditions.

Clearly, where we disagree is not as regards the past
achievements of protection or the need to preserve as far as
possible the employment already secured but as regards the
contribution which the continuance of high protection can
make to future national development. My view, as expressed
in the final paragraph of our memorandum, is that a
progressive lowering of tariffs is necessary for our economic
progress regardless of what is happening in the outside
world and is all the more necessary in view of the current
movement in Europe towards freer trade and the increased
competition to which this will give rise. This proposition
rests on the indisputable principle that the future expansion
of industry here is almost entirely dependent on attracting
external demand and that this in turn depends on a general
improvement in efficiency which cannot be expected if high
protection is maintained. Breaking into export markets means
giving priority to considerations of cost and quality, in the

[83]

recognition that employment can be expanded only if efficient production for export is built up. Change is inseparable from progress. Nobody suggests that we should sacrifice an existing industry merely to make it possible for foreigners to sell here. But we cannot develop and at the same time freeze the present industrial set-up. We must be prepared to scrap as well as build. Progress involves getting out of unprofitable lines as well as into profitable ones and the test of "profitability" in this connexion is the ability to sell in export markets.

The need for modification of the policy of protection is already widely accepted. To show that my arguments are not heterodox, may I quote the following passage from paragraph 99 of the Government's White Paper "Programme for Economic Expansion":

> "Bearing in mind that the only scope for substantial expansion lies in the production of goods for sale on export markets, it is clear that there can be no place for weak or inefficient industries. Even where only the home market is involved, it must be accepted that such industries place a burden on the economy generally and render other industries less able to meet foreign competition. Hence it must now be recognised that protection can no longer be relied upon as an automatic weapon of defence and it will be the policy in future *in the case of new industries* to confine the grant of tariff protection to cases in which it is clear that the industry will, after a short initial period, be able to survive without protection. The rules of the Free Trade Area will require a gradual and systematic reduction in *existing* tariffs".

It is true that the Free Trade Area then envisaged has not come into being but the Taoiseach, in concluding the adjournment debate on Government policy on 11th December last, stated:

> "The world trend however is towards freer trade and we must not blink our eyes to it. The Common Market is already making gestures towards a world agreement. Whatever may be the outcome of the negotiations with

Britain or the EFTA or anyone else, we must face up to the fact of our having to reduce our protective measures at some time and not too far ahead at that. Indeed, there is a case for doing it in our own interests apart from external arrangements. Everybody concerned, whether in management or as workers, in industry must face up to that prospect and prepare for it".

I need not quote again from the recent pamphlet of the National Council of the Federation of Irish Industries, where the imminent necessity for progressive reduction of protection, leading eventually to free trade, is recognised and it is claimed that Irish industry is sufficiently strong and adaptable to meet the situation successfully.

Surely we should take advantage of this progressive attitude? It would, to my mind, be bad administration to miss so good an opportunity of furthering the long-term national interest. Industry has been keyed up to expect progressive reductions in tariffs. The upward movement in industrial exports is a source of confidence. Participation in some form of free trade arrangement is the expected and natural context in which to set these reductions; as we have already pointed out, this will secure some payment or return for what it would be advantageous for us to do of our own accord. The merits of "going it alone", though real, would not, I fear, be so widely understood. The opportunity for independent action has existed for a long time, without being realised in practice. It is over a decade since your Department felt it necessary to draw up legislation to force the pace of progress in industrial efficiency. The legislation was not proceeded with. Responsibility for making periodic reviews of existing tariffs was later imposed on the Industrial Development Authority but these reviews have been infrequent and very few tariffs have been reduced. There can be no doubt that an externally-applied discipline, provided it is not too severe, will arouse less opposition, appear less discriminatory, and be more effective than a system operated entirely at the discretion of the domestic administration. The best way to get costs down to competitive levels is to face industrialists with the *certainty* that tariffs are going to be lowered. In their present mood and in an external trade relationship, I believe they will accept this pressure and react favourably to it.

A positive policy of tariff reduction, coupled with appropriate State aid for adaptation and modernisation, is to be preferred to an attempt, which I think must fail, to develop industry under the quasi-permanent shelter of protection. I cannot see any hope even of maintaining present output and employment on the basis of costs which will tend to become less and less competitive according as other countries realise more of the advantages of specialisation and scale. That is why I said, most deliberately, in my letter of 22 December to Cremin:

> "In considering the possible adverse effects of removal of protection, let us not forget the undoubtedly adverse consequences of being left stranded on a high and narrow protectionist plateau on which acceptable living standards could be provided only temporarily and for a diminishing number of our people".

For convenience of reference, I have appended a summary of my main propositions. So far as these are not accepted and it is contended that the progressive lowering of protective tariffs ought not or need not be used as a stimulus to increased efficiency, it is necessary to show cause for expecting that, in the absence of this stimulus, industrial development will provide a satisfactory increase in employment and living standards and even that the existing inadequate level of industrialisation can be maintained.

Yours sincerely,
T.K. WHITAKER

c.c.  Mr. Ó Muimhneacháin
     Mr. Cremin
     Mr. Nagle
     Mr. McElligott[20] } with copies of correspondence of
     Dr. McCarthy    } 22, 23 and 24 December

---

20  James J. McElligott (1893–1974), Secretary, Department of Finance (1927–53), Governor, Central Bank of Ireland (1953–60).

## SUMMARY OF PROPOSITIONS

1. Industrial production for a home market of the present size offers very little further scope for increased income or employment.

2. Progress in raising national income and employment (and home market purchasing power) depends henceforth on producing more for sale abroad.

3. Over a wide field, selling more abroad depends on increased efficiency of production, reflected in better quality and/or lower costs.

4. Shortlived though our enjoyment of protection may be as compared with other countries, we now have to make headway in export markets against the products of countries which are progressively dispensing with protection and putting themselves in a position to realise further economies of specialisation and scale.

5. In these circumstances, we must accelerate our efforts to catch up in efficiency and competitiveness.

6. The maintenance of a high level of protection will exert a retarding rather than an accelerating influence.

7. While it is proper to have regard to the risks for existing industries which the scaling down of protection will involve, the national interest requires a rapid expansion of industrial output mainly for sale abroad in increasingly competitive markets and this expansion can be achieved only on the basis of increased efficiency, which itself can be secured on the scale and in the time required only through the discipline of a gradual lowering of protection (such as participation in free trade arrangements must entail), accompanied by appropriate State aid for adaptation and modernisation.

## J.C.B. MacCarthy to T.K. Whitaker, 5 January 1960

Dear Whitaker,
Many thanks for your letter of 31st December.

Bearing in mind that our terms of reference are to prepare a memorandum on the implications of our joining EFTA (or entering a Free Trade arrangement with Britain) on terms similar to those agreed for Portugal, and on the minimum quid pro quo which would be acceptable from Britain in return for our so doing, I am reluctant to enter into arguments at this stage as to the relevant weight to be given to the various implications. I think the "dialogue" has been useful, however, and we will include among the implications the views you hold on the salutariness and likely outcome of tariff reductions. But we shall have to qualify the forecast by reference to the views we hold on the dangers inherent in such reductions. It is the overall advantage to the economy that must be the deciding factor and we can best consider this when the pros and cons have been clearly stated and evaluated.

So far as manufacturing industry is concerned, I am afraid I could never agree that the introduction of an externally-applied discipline of tariff reductions would be sufficient justification in itself for entering a free trade association. We know enough to realise that there would be consequent losses of industrial production and employment which would be warranted only if we got an adequate quid pro quo on the agricultural side. EFTA (excluding Britain) offers no worthwhile opportunities to us on the industrial side and the Department of Agriculture feels the same way about agricultural products.

Neither could I ever agree that it is realistic to visualise in the free trade context (whether with Britain or EFTA) a "rapid expansion of industrial output". The one thing I think to be quite certain is that there would not be a rapid expansion.

On the contrary, there would be a contraction and it would only be in the course of time, if at all, that the contraction of industrial production resulting from the losses in the home market could be redressed by increased sales abroad and only later still that the increased sales abroad could sustain a level of production exceeding the present level. I thought that this was understood all along and is indeed one of our strong points in looking for a substantial quid pro quo.

I am glad to know from your letter that you agree:

(a) that the risks for existing industries must not be understated in the memorandum (there is no danger of overstatement);

(b) that the discipline of tariff reductions in any external association must be "not too severe";

(c) that we can look for better terms than Portugal; and

(d) that appropriate State aid for adaptation and modernisation would be forthcoming if tariff reductions were imposed.

On the question of understatement of the risks to our existing industries, I must beg you to bear in mind that we are a very small country industrially and that we are on the doorstep of a very big industrial producer. That, to my mind, puts us in a special position and it would be far from realistic to close one's eyes to the fact. I have pointed out so often that I must apologise for reiterating that, if the protective barriers were lowered sufficiently, British manufacturers could put enough goods in here in next to no time to create havoc for our existing industries; and if we get down to hard brass tacks, as we should, we must recognise that the first result of a falling off in demand and of goods remaining unsold in factories is short-time working or closing down.

It may be decided for the greater good of the community as a whole to face the risks if an insurance is provided in the form of concessions in some other field; but I do not think it is realistic to think that we could assume externally-applied obligations without positive concessions in some other field; nor can the Department of Industry and Commerce advise whether these risks should be taken unless the minimum countervailing concessions are evaluated so that the balance of advantage can be seen.

There is no disagreement at all between your Department and mine as to what the objective is – an expansion of production and of exports – and there is no failure on the part of this Department to take cognisance of the Government's White Paper; the particular paragraph you quote from that Paper was written in this Department, if I mistake not.

We deem it to be our duty, however, to state the risks as we see them and I think we see them realistically. In so stating the risks we are not, as I have already said, taking up any *non possumus* attitude or saying that industrial protection must be retained if it can be shown that the same level of employment can be maintained by some other means.

I recognise the force of the comment you made to Cremin on the possibility of "being left stranded on a high and narrow protectionist plateau on which acceptable living standards could be provided only temporarily and for a diminishing number of our people". It is at least equally important, on the other hand, that we should not so minimise the risks of "Free Trade" as to obscure the possibility that the plateau or whatever replaces it would be occupied by a diminished number of our people even though their living standards, because there were fewer of them, might be enhanced. We must remember that, as Cremin pointed out, increased emigration would, in our circumstances, be an almost inevitable consequence of reduction of industrial employment.

Yours sincerely,
J.C.B. MacCARTHY

**T.K. Whitaker to J.C.B. MacCarthy, 7 January 1960**

Dear MacCarthy,

Thank you for your letter of 5th January.

It will, I think, help towards a clear statement of differences in the draft Memorandum which is in preparation if I make a few final observations:

(1)  The propositions summarised in my letter to you of 31st December, 1959, stand as a reasoned argument in support of a systematic, *unilateral* lowering of tariffs in the interests of industrial efficiency and national progress (whether rapid or slow).

(2)  I have argued that the benefit of joining some form of free trade association is that *some* quid pro quo is obtained for what it would be advantageous for us to do of our own accord. This means that I would not think it appropriate to fuss about the adequacy of any particular quid pro quo, though naturally I would take all I could get.

(3)  The sole benefit of joining a free trade area would not be the introduction of an externally-applied discipline of tariff reductions. Other benefits would be the reduction of tariffs against us by large importing countries at a more rapid rate for most goods than our own reductions – thus reducing our competitive disadvantage. Increased efficiency and drive, helped by tax concessions and other State aids, should enable our industries to gain more by expansion of exports than they would lose in the home market. Our industrial exports to Continental Europe have increased appreciably in recent years and it seems defeatist to refuse to see the possibility of worthwhile markets in EFTA.

(4)  If, however, you keep on saying that there are no worthwhile prospects for expansion of industrial exports to EFTA, you must be pressed for an answer to the following questions:

[91]

(a) whether this pessimism is due to the non-competitive character of most of Irish industrial production;

(b) how it is proposed to overcome this, if the discipline of gradual tariff reduction is not applied; and

(c) what grounds there are for expecting even that existing industrial output and employment can be maintained (not to speak of expanded) unless industry is somehow made to become more efficient in the near future.

(5) The risks for existing industries in the gradual withdrawal of protection could be overstated if due weight were not given to the risks (of growing non-competitiveness, wider disparities in real wages, and reduced sales and employment opportunities) involved in not taking such action. I think you recognise this in the final paragraph of your letter. The interpolation of the words "there is no danger of overstatement" at (a) of your summary of what I am supposed to have agreed to is inadvertent but rather amusing.

(6) As regards (c) on page 2 of your letter, what I said was "we can, if we wish, look for better terms than Portugal ... but do not let us forget that protection will not of itself sell our goods". How onerous the Portuguese terms would be for us has yet to be established.

(7) My remarks as summarised at (d) of your letter were in the context of general and systematic tariff reductions.

Despite your rather forbidding reiteration of "I could never agree", I have not abandoned hope of persuading you to see matters from a dynamic rather than a static viewpoint. However, let us wait now until the draft of the Memorandum is available!

Yours sincerely,
T.K. WHITAKER

cc. Mr. Ó Muimhneacháin, Mr. Cremin, Mr. Nagle, Mr. McElligott, Mr. McCarthy

*J.C.B. MacCarthy to T.K. Whitaker, 9 January 1960*

Dear Whitaker,

Thanks for your letter of the 7th January, though it grieves me to note that our exchange of correspondence seems to have done little to bring the discussion down to earth.

The view point expressed in your letter that our industries would gain more from expanded exports than they would lose in the home market, and that there is no need to fuss about getting an adequate quid pro quo for joining either EFTA or Britain in a free trade association, is so far removed from our viewpoint that I agree there is no point in continuing the correspondence.

Yours sincerely,
J.C.B. MACCARTHY

## T.K. Whitaker to J.C.B. MacCarthy, 11 January 1960

Dear MacCarthy,

I suppose I am entitled to the last word in our correspondence about the Reasons for Reducing Protection. I am sorry it must be that I cannot accept the second paragraph of your letter of 9th January as being a fair or reasonable summary of the views expressed in my previous letters.

Yours sincerely,
T.K. WHITAKER

# 4 The sequel

The 1958 Programme for Economic Expansion provided a psychological as well as an economic boost at a time of buoyancy in world trade, so that the 1960s became a decade of unprecedented average annual growth of 4%. A thorough review of industrial efficiency was undertaken at the start of the decade. Special grants, loans and tax incentives were provided to encourage firms to modernise and adapt to competitive trading conditions. Tariffs were even lowered unilaterally. Foreign firms were offered generous grants, on top of tax advantages, to set up here and export their output. The idea of joining EFTA was dropped. When, in July 1961, Britain first applied to join the EEC, we did so simultaneously but had to join the British on the sidelines when President de Gaulle vetoed their application. A Free Trade Area Agreement was concluded with Britain at the end of 1965 and, when the British application to join the EEC was renewed in May 1967, we re-applied also. Detailed negotiations were successfully completed in the 1970 to 1972 period, accession instruments were signed in January 1972, and Ireland, with strong public approval in a referendum, became a member simultaneously with Britain on 1 January 1973.

The course of our "tortuous path" towards EEC membership is traced in Denis Maher's book of that title, published by the IPA in 1986.

Unfortunately, in a perverse reaction to the oil crises of the 1970s and a mistaken dash, under the 1977 Manifesto, to full employment, excessive foreign indebtedness was incurred which impeded development. Fortunately, the return to wise economic policies in the later 1980s enabled us to regain our Paradise Lost and ushered in the phenomenal success of the 1990s, a decade in which real living standards increased by 50%. The heavy emigration of the 1950s had reduced the population to the lowest-ever level of 2.8 million in 1961 but the tide was already turning. By 1966 a rise of 66,000 was recorded and we have now topped 4 million, net immigration having replaced net emigration.